CW00828132

Faces, Cases and Places

Faces, Cases and Places

Memoirs by

Fatayi Williams

Nigerian Jurist

London
BUTTERWORTHS
1983

England	Butterworth & Co (Publishers) Ltd
	88 Kingsway, London WC2B 6AB
Australia	Butterworths Pty Ltd
	271–273 Lane Cove Road, North Ryde, NSW 2113
	Also at Melbourne, Brisbane, Adelaide and Perth
Canada	Butterworth & Co (Canada) Ltd
	2265 Midland Avenue, Scarborough, Ont M1P 4S1
	Butterworth & Co (Western Canada) Ltd
	409 Granville Street, Ste 856, Vancouver, BC V6C 1T2
New Zealand	Butterworths of New Zealand Ltd
	33–35 Cumberland Place, Wellington
Singapore	Butterworth & Co (Asia) Pte Ltd
	Crawford Post Office Box 770
	Singapore 9119
United States of America	Mason Publishing Company
	Finch Building, 366 Wacouta Street,
	St Paul, Minn 55101
	Butterworth (Legal Publishers) Inc
	160 Roy Street, Ste 300, Seattle, Wash 98109
	Butterworth (Legal Publishers) Inc
	381 Elliot Street, Newton, Upper Falls, Mass 02164

© Fatayi Williams 1983

ISBN 0 406 51477 1

Typeset by Phoenix Photosetting, Chatham
Printed in Great Britain by Mackays of Chatham Ltd

TO IRENE

Who has shared all my trials and tribulations

Preface

I grew up in a household oriented towards private enterprise and self reliance but with a deep sense of service to the community, justice and fair play. I believe in equal opportunities for all Nigerians irrespective of religious or ethnic origin. I believe in merited privilege, the privilege of enjoying the fruits of one's labours. Inherited wealth, particularly on a large scale is, however, indefensible. In most cases, it leads to a life of dedicated indolence. I also believe uncompromisingly in the rule of law and that once the rule of law is jettisoned, anarchy will be the sole beneficiary. Like that greatest of Americans, Abraham Lincoln, I subscribe to the thought that –

'You cannot bring about prosperity by discouraging thrift;

You cannot help the wage-earner by pulling down the wage-payer;

You cannot further the brotherhood of man by encouraging class hatred;

You cannot help the poor by destroying the rich;

You cannot keep out of trouble by spending more than you earn;

You cannot build character and courage by taking away a man's initiative;

You cannot help men permanently by doing for them what they could and should do for themselves.'

My whole life is a reflection of these guiding principles. The story which I am about to tell is how those principles have affected and shaped my life. If the next generation of Nigerians can benefit from this account of my life which spans both the colonial and the post-independence era, then my labour would not have been in vain.

The book is intended to contain a record of the strains and stresses of my times, including a record of the town where I was born and the places where I worked or which I visited. It is also intended to assist the reader to have a descriptive glimpse at the faces, the lives and the careers of people who, at various stages, have influenced my life or my attitude to life and events. Contact with some of them has helped to shape my character and to strengthen my faith in the rule of law and the independence of the judiciary.

Unlike the cases which come before us daily in the Supreme Court, the few cases I have referred to in the text are not those in which dry or profound legal principles are considered and adjudicated upon. They are, in the main, cases with a strong human element relative to the prevailing circumstances in a developing country such as Nigeria. They deal with human weaknesses in the quest for power or justice in a country which is still finding her feet in a confused and violent world, where power still corrupts and where the rule of law is still being gradually accepted especially by the powerful.

My efforts in putting my thoughts together in this book would not have materialised but for the unflagging help and support of my personal secretary, Mrs Vivienne Nnoka, who spent most of her off-duty hours going through all the relevant documents and typing the manuscript. I am also grateful to my son, Babatunde Fatayi-Williams, for reading through the typescript and calling my attention to errors which I had overlooked. Finally, I am grateful to my publishers who have shown great efficiency and have been tolerant of any delay on my part.

A Fatayi-Williams
Chief Justice's Chambers
Supreme Court of Nigeria
Lagos
July 1982

Contents

Illustrations

13. The three sons of the Fatayi-Williams, l. to r. – Oladele, aged 4 years, Babatunde, aged 10 years and Alan, aged 8 years

14. Visit to Nigeria of the Colonial Secretary, Oliver Lyttelton (later Lord Chandos). Front row l. to r. – the Governor, A. Odulana, Oliver Lyttelton, A. Reffell, A. Steward. Back row l. to r. – J. K. Randle, Name Unknown, Alex Oni, A. Fatayi-Williams, S. Nottidge, J. K. Agbaje

15. Chief S. O. Adebo, Mrs Morrison and A. Fatayi-Williams at Constitutional Conference held in London in August/September, 1957

16. Conference on the Problems of Federalism held in Lagos in March 1960. Sitting in the front row are: 3rd from left, the late Sir Louis Mbanefo, 5th from left, Lord Diplock, Chief F. R. A. Williams, Lord Denning and Sir Adetokunbo Ademola. Fatayi-Williams is in the back row 5th from left between Mike Winton and H. H. Marshall

17. Pilgrimage to Mecca 1961. L. to r. – Dr A. Atta, A. Fatayi-Williams and Dr A. Jinadu

18. A. Fatayi-Williams on appointment as High Court Judge in October, 1960

19. Opening of Assizes in Benin, 1961

20. A. Fatayi-Williams and Fani-Kayode in Ibadan, 1965

21. Ports Arbitration Tribunal, 1972. L. to r. – the late Louis Edet, A. Fatayi-Williams and Gus Ehren in Calabar

22. Irene Fatayi-Williams with Justice G. S. Sowemimo of the Supreme Court and Justice A. Belgore, then Chief Judge of Plateau State

23. A. Fatayi-Williams as Supreme Court Justice in ceremonial robes, 1975

24. Some Justices at a drinks party in the premises of the former Chief Justice of Nigeria, Sir Darnley Alexander. L. to r. – Justice A. Obaseki of the Supreme Court, Justice A. Belgore, then Chief Judge of Plateau State, Justice A. Fatayi- Williams of the Supreme Court, Sir Darnley Alexander, Justice M. Bello of the Supreme Court, Justice A. Adefarasin, Chief Judge of Lagos State and Justice C. Idigbe of the Supreme Court

25. At the International Conference in Manila, Philippines, 1977. L. to r. – President Marcos of the Philippines, Mrs Marcos,

Justice Fatayi-Williams, Chief Justice Fred Castro of the
Philippines, and a Justice of the Philippines Supreme Court

26. L. to r. – Chief Justice Fatayi-Williams, Mrs Fatayi-Williams,
Lord Widgery (formerly Lord Chief Justice of England) and
Lady Widgery on a boat cruise around Sydney Harbour,
Australia, during an International Conference of Appellate
Judges held in Sydney, Australia in June, 1980. Lord Widgery
died a year later in 1981

27. The Hon. Chief Justice Fatayi-Williams in his Chambers in
the Supreme Court, Lagos, December, 1979

28. Chief Justice Fatayi-Williams inspecting the Guard of Honour
mounted by the Nigeria Police before the opening of the All
Nigeria Magistrates' Conference in Ilorin, capital of Kwara
State, November, 1980

1 Early days

My grandfather, Seidu Jabita Williams, was a a highly successful merchant in Lagos. As proof of his success, he built himself an attractive storey-house at No 19, Bishop Street (now known as Alhaji Issa Williams Street after my late father). This house abuts the family compound which is at No 19A, Bishop Street. My father, who was born at No 19, Bishop Street in 1896, lived there with my mother whom he married in 1915. I was also born there on 22 October 1918. Other members of the family, including my grandfather and his four wives, also lived there.

My grandfather was born in Lagos around 1858 to Osineye, a native of Ljebu-Ode, who had earlier migrated to Lagos in 1837 where he lived at Olowogbowo until his death. He attended the Olowogbowo Wesleyan School (now the Methodist School) where he stayed until he reached Standard Four Primary. He then started to trade for his late brother Jacob Aleshinloye Williams for whom he went on several trips to Dahomey and the Gold Coast. Later, with his cousin Brimah Williams, he was put in charge of the main shop of Jacob Aleshinloye Williams. A few years later, he left this shop and started business jointly with Brimah Williams under the business name of S & B Williams.

The business prospered up to the time of the trade depression which followed in the wake of the First World War (1914–1918). They both lost a lot of money during the depression. The storey-house at No 19,

1

Bishop Street had to be sold to pay off creditors. Nevertheless, at the time of his death in 1949, Seidu still owned the large family compound at No 19A, Alhaji Issa Williams Street, Lagos, and also other properties which he had developed and occupied with his family at Nos 13 and 15, Bankole Street nearby and at Alakoro, Marina. He also owned a large farmland at Ipaja, near Agege, where his children and grandchildren used to spend their school holidays.

Seidu Williams was one of the racing barons of Lagos. The mere mention of his name in racing circles at the time would bring to mind some of his famous mounts such as 'Ikorodu' and 'Idowa'. 'Ikorodu' won the coveted Governor's Cup in Lagos on at least three occasions. Up to the time of his death in 1949, my grandfather was also a prominent member of the Lagos Central Mosque, the Ilu Committee, and the Olowogbowo Council. At the turn of the century, the Ilu Committee was the Governor's main and highly prestigious advisory body.

Seidu Williams had many children among whom was my father, the late Alhaji Issa Williams, a prosperous merchant after whom Alhaji Issa Williams Street is named. The late Alhaji Issa Williams was also blessed with many children, among whom are Dr Wahab Williams, a medical practitioner, Professor S K Taiwo Williams, one time Professor and Dean of the Faculty of Agriculture and Deputy Vice Chancellor at the University of Ife, and now Professor of Agriculture, University of Ibadan, M O K Williams, a Permanent Secretary in the Office of the Secretary to the Executive President of Nigeria, Samie Williams, a chartered accountant and deputy managing director of Guinness (Nigeria) Ltd, Rasheed Williams, an insurance executive and managing director of Lombard Insurance Co of Nigeria Ltd, Ridwan Williams, an automobile engineer, and the author.

Curiously enough, it is the daughters of the late

Alhaji Issa Williams who are merchants in their own right who still carry on this family tradition with commendable success.

My paternal grandmother, Sabalimotu Williams who was also known as 'Iya Idoluwo', was one of the four wives of Seidu Williams. Born during the reign of King Dosunmu of Lagos, she died aged about 100 in 1969. Grandmother's father was Amidu, a great Muslim scholar from the Idoluwo area of Lagos. Amidu's father came originally from Sierra Leone. He was a mulatto and friend of Bashorun Carew of Lagos. On his arrival in Lagos, he bought Amidu's mother, who came from Offa, as a slave, freed and then married her. Sabalimotu's mother was Iyanotu, a daughter of Oshorun Eyidan from Imahin and Rakia, a Nupe woman from Okene. Oshorun Eyidan came to Lagos with Oba Akinsemoyin and traded for him with the Brazilians. He was later one of the warriors of the Obas of Lagos during the Olomiro War, the Afesegbojo War, and Akitoye the Third's War in which he died from war wounds.

I was my mother's first son and second child. She also bore my father two daughters and five other sons all of whom now hold prominent positions in Nigeria's public and commercial life.

Large families confer a certain status on the men in their communities. They have always been regarded as a blessing, presumably because of the high infant mortality rate. The land in Nigeria, being fertile, makes it possible for the extra children, who cost nothing to feed, to work on the farm.

Nowadays, however, the economic realities of living in an increasingly consumer-oriented, urbanised and western-educated society has tended to undermine the practice of polygamy. Be that as it may, at the time when I was born, polygamy was more the rule rather than the exception. I grew up in a happily polygamous household although I am now equally happily married to one wife.

As a result of the trade recession which followed the

3

boom of the First World War, my grandfather got heavily into debt. The main house at No 19, Bishop Street had to be sold although the family compound at No 19A, is still part of the family holding today. Grandfather, and most of the members of his family, including my father, mother and their children, moved into a much smaller house at No 13, Bankole Street nearby. This was where I and my brothers and sisters spent our childhood days until 1938 when we moved into the storey-house at No 17, Bankole Street which my father had then bought. Although living was rather cramped at No 13, Bankole Street, it was, nevertheless, a happy home, full of fun and adventure.

The family are all devout Muslims. In the early part of the nineteen-twenties, my father joined the Ahmadiyya Movement-in-Islam, a Muslim sect which has its origin in Rabwah in the Punjab. Its main religious belief, which differentiates it from other Muslim sects, is that its adherents believe in the advent of the Mahdi (the Messiah) in India. This decision was most unpopular with a large section of the Seidu Williams' family. Despite my tender age, I was well aware of the family grumblings and disapproval. Friends and other relatives also disapproved of my father's action. Like a true Williams, however, he stuck to his belief although he later severed all connections with the headquarters of the Movement in Pakistan.

After his conversion, I was sent, following a short period at the local Arabic school, where I can only recollect that I learnt very little arabic and even less about reading the Koran, to the Talimul-Islam Ahmadiyya Primary School near Aroloya Street in Lagos. The distance did not worry me much because my mother's family house at Garba Square, Ita Akanni, where both my maternal grandfather and my grandmother lived, was on my way to school and I called on them regularly. On such occasions, I was treated to a good meal and given a few pennies. Because I am

4

blessed with a fairly retentive memory, school, from the very beginning, was fun. I worked hard and played equally hard.

I stayed at that school until 1929 when I gained admission into standard two at the Wesleyan Boys' High School, Lagos (now the Methodist Boys' High School), a school which my father had attended when he was young.

I recall an early incident which might have influenced my later decision to read law. One day, when I was about seven years of age, my grandfather called me and asked me to accompany him to see his lawyer, the late Eric Moore, at Tinubu Street. Grandfather went in a cart. Because the roads in Lagos in those days were not only few, narrow and very bad, the Marina, Broad Street, and Victoria Street (now renamed Nnamdi Azikiwe Street) being the only roads of any size worth mentioning, the cart, which was used exclusively by the more affluent members of the community, was very much in evidence. A small, open two-wheeled vehicle similar to a Japanese rickshaw and drawn by one man, the cart had room for only one or two persons. I sat on the floor at the bottom of the cart on the day I went with my grandfather to see Mr Eric Moore. Grandfather sat on the small upholstered platform.

On reaching Eric Moore's office, at about 4.30 in the afternoon, the clerk told us that his employer was resting. We therefore waited in the office for him. At about 6.30, the great man, who was then one of the top lawyers in the country and a member of the Legislative Council, came down and explained to grandfather that he could not see him then and that he would have to come back another time. My grandfather grumbled all the way home, complaining that he did not understand why his lawyer, whom he had paid handsomely, should treat him like that. I felt so sorry for the old man and thought that if he had had a son who was himself a lawyer, he would not have suffered what he rightly considered an unmerited humiliation.

During the school holidays I used to visit the Law Courts in Tinubu Square to watch the proceedings. My interest in the Courts started with my friendship with Chief Remi Fani-Kayode and Adelumola Ibikunle Akitoye late in 1934, when I joined the Green Triangle Club. This was a social club of young men and women, founded for the purpose of raising funds through dances and football matches organised by the club to help socially and physically handicapped children and young people in Lagos.

Chief Fani-Kayode's father read law at Selwyn College, Cambridge and was later called to the Bar in the Middle Temple in London. A brilliant advocate of countrywide repute, we young schoolboys of that time enjoyed the treat of watching him argue in court. After a number of visits to the Courts during the course of which I watched Mr Adedapo Kayode and other brilliant advocates perform, I decided that my career lay at the Bar. What a hope, especially in those days when the highest post that had ever been achieved by a Nigerian was that of Police Magistrate at the St Anna Magistrate's Court near Tinubu Square! Mr Olumuyiwa Jibowu, an Oxford graduate and another brilliant and hardworking lawyer, was that lonely Nigerian. He was later to attain high judicial office as Sir Olumuyiwa Jibowu, the Chief Justice of Western Nigeria.

The Methodist Boys' High School opened up new interests for me. Schoolwork came easily to me and my interest in learning and, indeed, in games, never flagged throughout the nine happy years I spent in that school under the headmastership, first of the late Mr J T Jackson, a dedicated teacher and scientist, and then of Mr Bandele Oyediran who later held high public office as the Nigerian High Commissioner in Sierra Leone. I left school in December 1938, having passed the Cambridge School Certificate Examinations with exemption from the London Matriculation Examination.

Two years before I left school early in 1936, a young

Nigerian returned to Lagos after studying in the United States of America where he had taken degrees in journalism and political science. Before returning to Nigeria, he had worked in the Gold Coast for a brief period as editor of the African Morning Post, in the course of which he narrowly escaped conviction for sedition. On his return to Nigeria, he started a newspaper. For the first time he gave Nigerian youth a purpose in life embodied in a public lecture delivered by him soon after his return to Lagos.

What that young Nigerian preached to us in the course of that memorable lecture was amply summarised by him in his book *My Odyssey*. The summary reads –

'Then I appealed to the audience to look round the world and observe the widespread revolt of the youth-in-mind against the cant and hypocrisy of the day. There was need for a new approach to the problems of Africa, I urged, as I proceeded to demonstrate how a new Africa could emerge from the debris of the old.

The realisation of a new Africa was possible, according to my thesis, by the Africans cultivating spiritual balance, practicalising social regeneration, realising economic determinism, becoming mentally emancipated, and ushering in a political resurgence. By spiritual balance, I meant freedom of expression and respect for the opinion of others. Social regeneration implied the treatment of all Africans as brothers and sisters, irrespective of tribe, so as to crystallise a sense of oneness and identity of community interest. No longer should Africans draw a line of distinction, based on tribal or linguistic factors, but they should appreciate the universal affinity of all African peoples.

By mental emancipation, I meant the eradication of fear in the mental make-up of the African. I urged my audience to emancipate themselves from the servitude

7

of an inferiority complex, and substitute therefore a sort of psychological aggression. I adduced evidence to prove the mental and physical equality of Africans with the other races of mankind. I referred to the role played by Africans in ancient history: how the Greek literati portrayed the progenitors of Africans as gods and objects of beauty, and how they connected the black race with all that was noble, godly, and virtuous.

I mentioned the role of the black Ethiopians of the xxvth dynasty in Egyptian history in 663 BC. I narrated how the blacks from the Sudan, Napata and Meroe domiciled in Egypt, miscegenated with Egyptians and influenced the various dynasties of Egypt.

Then I wended my way through the corridors of time and told the story of the African in world history, spotlighting the immortal exploits of the black Duke of Florence, St Benedict the Black, Hannivalov of Russia, Amo, Alexandre Dumas, Chevalier de St George, Toussaint l'Ouverture, Dessalines, Phyllis Wheatley, Benjamin Russwurm, Booker T Washington, George Washington Carver, and other great men and women who, in various fields of human endeavour, physical and mental, had demonstrated the capacity of the black peoples.

I suggested that, if Africans could leave their native haunts and proceed to Europe or America to rub shoulders with the best intellectuals produced by these countries and even at times, surpass them, this proved conclusively that not only was the African the equal of any race on earth, but he was also superior to some of the representatives of the various races of mankind. Therefore, I urged my hearers to be up and doing, because the realisation of an independent political existence (which, in my speech, I identified as political resurgence), presumed the four steps outlined by me, so as to concretise a trained mind, a sense of oneness, economic security, and an aristocracy of intelligence.

I concluded as follows: 'Where you have people whose thinking has evolved beyond the primal stage and who allow reason to control their thoughts; where you have people who appreciate their common affinity and live in a co-operative spirit; where you have people who are economically secure, individually and collectively; where you have people, who are creative factors in the social and material cultures of mankind, you cannot keep them politically subservient indefinitely. That is the substance of our revolt against the *status quo*. It shall be the basis of my mission and become a crusade for national freedom and the liberation of Africa from the manacles of European imperialism. God helping me, Nigeria shall be free and out of the struggle shall emerge a new Africa.".'

The lecture not only had an electrifying effect on all the young men of my time, it also set Nigeria ablaze. From then on, many young men were determined, by hook or by crook, to go abroad and return with the necessary qualifications to free our country from the shackles of colonial rule. The person who fired our imagination so resolutely is none other than Dr Nnamdi Azikiwe (popularly known as 'Zik'). He eventually played a crucial political role during Nigeria's post-war reconstruction. Later, he became the first indigenous Governor-General of Nigeria when the country became independent. In 1963, he became President of the Federal Republic of Nigeria, under the new Constitution by which Nigeria became a Republic.

Soon after I left school in 1938, rumours grew about the possibility of another world war. As a result, father advised me to take a job locally and see how the threat of war developed. In compliance, I joined the Medical Department as a third-class clerk on 36 pounds per annum, a handsome salary for a junior clerk in those days! When war was eventually declared on Germany

9

nine months later, in September 1938, I became restless thinking that my opportunity for higher education abroad might slip away. At that time, apart from the discredited Higher College at Yaba, where the qualifications awarded were only locally recognised, there was no other institution of higher learning in Nigeria. Certainly no educational institution made provision for the study of law.

Eventually it became clear that the war would last longer than originally expected. Not surprisingly, we young men who were planning to go abroad became disenchanted with the intransigence of our parents. We decided to make plans for travelling abroad for further studies with or without our parents' approval. After all, Zik had made it on his own!

We formed a club in Lagos. We called it 'The Red Club', though it had nothing to do with communism. It was so named because we all wore distinctive red shirts at our monthly meetings when we considered plans for going in search of 'the golden fleece'. We were a small and select group, not more than nine in all, but all determined to make something of our lives. The members of the Club were Remi Fani-Kayode, T A Bank-Oki, Sonny Adewale (later known as 'The Boy is Good'), Afolabi Silva, Victor Haffner, the late Adeolu Allen, the late Magnus Macaulay, S K Domingo and the author. It could be said to our credit that we all left Nigeria as planned, and achieved what we set out to achieve. Fani-Kayode, Magnus Macaulay and I succeeded in getting into Cambridge where we each read law. After serving in the Royal Air Force, Adewale and Bank-Oki also read law in London. Haffner qualified in telecommunications while Allen and Silva also read law. Domingo studied mass communications.

2 In search of the Golden Fleece

Having heard from some unknown source about our plans, father called me one day in 1942, and said that I might as well start making arrangements for gaining admission to a British University. Unknown to him, I had already applied to Trinity Hall, University of Cambridge, and had been granted provisional admission provided I could pass a prescribed college entrance examination on arrival. Because of this, it did not take much time to get my papers and passport in order. I accordingly resigned my appointment with the Medical Department in June 1942, and booked my passage on one of the Elder Dempster ships to England.

Under the wartime conditions which obtained in Lagos in 1942, ships to England were few and their departure dates were irregular. Moreover, for security reasons, passengers were not given more than a few hours' notice of the time of embarkation. I eventually obtained a passage early in November 1942 on the *MV Stentor* (one of the ships chartered by Elder Dempster Lines, because they had, by then, lost most of their own shipping through enemy action). We left Lagos for Freetown where our ship joined a convoy of about 70 others. Some days after we left Freetown and in spite of all security precautions, sixteen out of the seventy ships were torpedoed on four consecutive nights. The *MV Stentor* was one of those sixteen ships. We were torpedoed at night in mid-Atlantic and in very cold weather about 500 miles off the Canary Islands and sank

11

within fifteen minutes. We lost everything except the pyjamas we were wearing in bed at the time of the attack. Through Allah's intervention, no doubt, all the Nigerians on board survived – although none of us knew this at the time because we were rescued in separate lifeboats. It was on our arrival later in the United Kingdom that we discovered we were all safe. I was eventually transferred from the lifeboat in which I was rescued into a corvette. About a week or two later, we were transferred to an American destroyer which was on its way to England from New York. I arrived at Liverpool in a sailor's uniform supplied to me by a kind crewman on the American destroyer, having lost everything I had brought out from Nigeria. The Liverpool branch of the Red Cross gave me an 'off-the-peg and try-it-on suit' in exchange for my uniform, a travelling warrant with which to travel by train to London and a one pound note for incidental expenses. I arrived at Euston Station, London, one night late in November 1942. It was very cold and foggy and there was total black-out. All I knew about London was that the West African Students' Union (WASU) was located in Camden Town. Soon I was all alone with an evil looking white man in a taxi in dark, cold, fog-ridden London, not knowing the cost of the fare let alone my own fate – and I had never seen a taximeter in my life! Appearances are, however, sometimes very deceptive. The taxi driver was very kind; he asked me a few questions and took me straight to WASU where I met the late Chief Ladipo Solanke who was then the manager and who received me with open arms. The fare charged by the taxi driver was reasonable and I had enough change for three days' meals at least. Money came from home a few days later after my parents had been informed of my safe arrival in London. As neither the name of the ship nor the names of survivors could be released to my parents at the time our ship was torpedoed, their ordeal must have been awful.

12

The WASU in London was glittering with talent in those days, buzzing with West African students – post-graduate and undergraduate – with political ambitions. There was Dr Adekoye Majekodunmi (now Chief Koye Majekodunmi) with the inspiring aura of a brilliant medical career in Dublin; Dr Udo Udoma (later Sir Udo Udoma of the Supreme Court of Nigeria and one-time Chairman of the Constituent Assembly which drafted the Constitution of the Second Republic) then a brilliant speaker with a Gold Medal for public speaking awarded by the Philosophical Society of Dublin University; Chief Rotimi Williams, preparing for his final bar examination, having taken a good Second Class Honours Degree from Selwyn College, Cambridge. There was also Joe Appiah from Ghana who later married the daughter of Sir Stafford Cripps, Chancellor of the Exchequer in the postwar Labour Government; Kamkam Boadu, also from Ghana, a Cambridge lawyer who, I gathered later, abandoned the law for commerce and industry. From Ghana also came Robert Gardner who later became an international statesman and the first Secretary-General of the Economic Commission for Africa. These are only a few of the brilliant young Africans I met at WASU in those days. WASU was at that time the powerhouse of West African politics.

Soon after my arrival in England I was admitted to University College Hospital with pneumonia and was not completely fit again until about March 1943. By then, it was too late for me to enrol at Cambridge for the academic year 1942–43. In June of that same year, I took the Trinity Hall entrance examination which I passed. I went up in the following October to read law.

Cambridge basks in history, ennobled by ancient stone and spires, lawns mowed and rolled for many centuries, pubs that would never dream of being modernised. The meadowland behind the colleges by the river, known as 'the Backs', is gloriously pastoral in

13

early June. The River Cam, with its slow, muddy waters, radiant along the 'Back' of Trinity Hall, seems to stand still. The town was in my time and I gather still is, the University. Then, battered bicycles and worn-out jackets with leather reinforcements on both elbows were in style. Undergraduates stalked about with an air of distinguished determination and sometimes arrogant self-confidence.

Trinity Hall, during my time, was Cambridge's premier law college. Over sixty per cent of the undergraduates there read law. Some of the best law tutors in Cambridge at the time were either fellows or dons there.

It must be remembered that, as a Nigerian fresh from West Africa I was unfamiliar with British manners, humour and mores. Nevertheless, the undergraduates at Trinity Hall accepted me as one of themselves. I made many friends there and I still see some of them when I go abroad. The undergraduates came from all over the world. I enjoyed, as a member of the College, a full and exhilarating social life. We often went to London together to see shows and exhibitions.

Cambridge was for me an ideal place to study. Students were treated as mature, responsible individuals. The underlying philosophy was, and still is, that if a student wanted education, he would obtain it without constant supervision. I recall my surprise that some of my tutors recommended that I should attend certain lectures and not bother about others. Even those that were recommended were not mandatory. One gained more from the supervision which was organised in small groups of five students than from lectures.

There was much emphasis on games at Trinity Hall, particularly on rowing, rugby and cricket. But no-one pushed or pressured you into playing any particular game. I played soccer for my College and obtained my colours for two years running. Lawrence Anionwu, another Nigerian who was also reading law, was the

14

Captain of the College team. He later joined the Nigerian Foreign Service and having served for some time as Nigeria's Ambassador to Italy, retired finally from the Service after serving as the Permanent Secretary in the Ministry of External Affairs. In addition to organised sports, students could enjoy games for their own sake. In this spirit, I used to swim during the summer months.

I soon realised that the responsibility for making a success or failure of my studies lay entirely with me. It was a powerful incentive and any serious student quickly developed the art of self-discipline. This helped me a lot in planning my schedule of work because, apart from my legal studies, I had so much general reading about life and about international affairs to do. Cambridge certainly opened new horizons of learning to me. Lectures and clubs could and did offer the broadest views of international politics and economics. My extra-curricular interest in these subjects turned into fascination. I was, therefore, able to absorb information quite readily. I developed an insatiable urge to read about the lives of great men who had made their impact either on world affairs or in their chosen fields of endeavour. I was, indeed, getting an education in the widest sense of the word.

There were quite a number of Nigerian students at Cambridge at the same time as I was up there. There was Chuku Nwapa, who later became the Federal Minister for Trade and Industries in the first ministerial government of 1953, at Selwyn College. Also at Selwyn were Mr Justice Akinkugbe of the Federal Court of Appeal, Mr Justice Gboyega Ademola, formerly of the Western State Court of Appeal, and Mr Felix Iheanacho, former Chairman of the East-Central State Public Service Commission. Chief Jerome Udoji, the late Magnus Macaulay, Dan Jumbo and I B Johnson were all up at King's while Mr Justice Chuba Ikpeazu was at St Catherine's College. Trinity College had Professor Saburi Biobaku, Professor E A Taiwo, Brigadier Austin Peters and Mr Joe Imoukhuede, one-time Secretary of the Mid-West State Government. Fani-Kayode was up at Downing and Lawrence Anionwu was reading law at Trinity Hall with me.

As it was wartime, some colleges in the University of London had been evacuated to Cambridge and as a result Nigerians were to be found who were taking degrees or diploma courses at King's College, the London School of Economics, University College and Queen Mary College, all constituent colleges of London University. Among these was Dr T O Elias, a former Chief Justice of Nigeria and now the President of the International Court at The Hague. Also in Cambridge were the late Raymond Njoku, Mr Justice Chike Idigbe of the Supreme Court of Nigeria, Gabriel Onyiuke, a senior advocate of Nigeria, and the late Nwabufor Uwechia.

In addition to the Nigerians, there were also other students from various parts of Africa up at Cambridge around this time. I clearly remember Frederick Mutesa (known popularly as 'King Freddie'), the Kabaka of Uganda who was at Magdalene College. Among the Ghanaians, were the Torto brothers at Queen Mary College (London), Chum Barima at Trinity, and Kamkam Boadu at Selwyn and Dr Davidson-Nicol from Sierra Leone was at Christ's.

The focal point for all West African students, and indeed for all African students, was the Cambridge branch of WASU. We met on Sundays once a month around tea-time in the rooms of a Ghanaian student from Queen's College. We drank tea and talked politics, both national and international. A favourite topic of discussion was the role which each of us would play in our countries' postwar development. When President Roosevelt of the United States announced his Atlantic Charter in 1944, in which he said that all countries had the right of self-determination, we were all greatly encouraged.

For me, the four years I spent at Cambridge were years of no regrets. I not only read law and enjoyed it, I also had plenty of time to catch up with my reading. I did not realise how ignorant I was about world affairs until I started reading books recommended to me by friends. I read avidly and talked at length over tea or coffee. There were many brilliant conversationalists at Cambridge in those days. In so far as the politics of de-colonisation were concerned, the Indian students were the most knowledgeable. The late Pandit Nehru was their hero. The complete freedom of India from British rule dominated their attitude to life and to contemporary events. I also learned a lot about British politics and about their past prime ministers and statesmen. American politics and institutions were also not left out of our discussions. I drank deep of the knowledge which my residence at Cambridge opened up to me. The weekly meeting of the Cambridge University Society for International Affairs (CUSIA), where brilliant and knowledgeable speakers from all over the United Kingdom came to talk to us, became to me a date that must be kept. As Trinity Hall was strongly in evidence at the Cambridge Union, I also attended the Union debates regularly although I did not once speak there. I was learning and in order to do this to my greatest advantage, I just looked, listened and appraised. Law Moots, in which those of us reading law took part in mock trials, were also regular features of life at Trinity Hall. As a matter of fact, in the Trinity Hall of those days, you either read, rowed or roamed. Roaming meant mixing freely with the international set of undergraduates from other colleges. Believe me, it was an education in itself learning about their countries, culture, problems, and way of life at first hand. Naturally, I read and roamed. The ability to mix freely with peoples of every race and nationality, which I cultivated in my undergraduate days at Cambridge, has stood me in good stead throughout my life.

17

Life was not, however, all work. We also drank beer and danced. At the 'May Balls' organised by the colleges during the early part of June, there would be champagne, beautiful girls, perfume and parties, with dancing in a marquee erected on the lawn. Usually an all-night affair, it would end with punting in boats up to 'The Orchard', a restaurant at the village of Granchester nearby, for breakfast, still attired in black-tie and evening dress. There was fun. There were also frolics. Mild misbehaviour was a recognised art-form. But the 'Bull-dogs' – the University policemen – were there to keep order and to see that nothing got out of hand.

I sat for my Tripos examination in May 1946. Being confident that I had not done too badly, I attended a number of May Balls. My cousin, Sir Mobolaji Bank-Anthony and his wife, Lande, who were both in England at the time, came up to Cambridge the day after I took my degree. We had lunch together and then went to the best photographers in town and had our photos taken. I was glad that at least two members of my family were around during this milestone in my career. Although I had taken my BA degree in Law, my father wanted me to stay up for another year and take the LLB degree which was, and still is, a postgraduate degree at Cambridge. I duly complied with his wish, stayed up for another year, and took the LLB degree in June 1947. I then went down to London for a holiday before facing the rigours of the Bar examinations. Incidentally, three years earlier, I had enrolled as a student of the Middle Temple in London where I had been eating the prescribed 'dinners' regularly. Since I had been exempted from the first part of the Bar examinations because of my grade in the Cambridge Tripos examinations, all I needed to do in order to qualify as a barrister, was to take and pass the final examination in the prescribed subjects. I passed the examination in May 1948. I was called to the Bar on 9 June 1948. The following day, I was married.

In London I first shared a spacious three-bedroom flat with Sonny Adewale and T A Bankole-Oki at No 30B, Lexham Gardens, Earls Court.

A few days after my arrival in London, I ran into Austen Peters, another friend from home, who was then doing his clinicals in one of the London hospitals and we decided to go to the British Council, then situated in Hanover Square, to find out what programme they had for students in London that summer. There I was introduced to a girl who was in charge of the Oxford and Cambridge desk. Her name was Irene Lofts. We talked to her about our requirements and she brought out brochures about lots of things going on in London for the benefit of foreign students. She made various suggestions and was extremely helpful. At the end of the interview, I tried to get a date out of her but she was reluctant to have anything to do with me, pleading work or previous engagements. But I was persistent. In the end, she ran out of excuses and gave me a date five weeks later to see 'The Best Years of Our Lives', a popular film then showing in London, to be followed by dinner. Fortunately for me, I went to see this film with another girlfriend, so when I met Irene again I had to confess to her that I had already seen the film and that I would rather we saw something else. She told me later that she was so flabbergasted about that candid confession that her interest in me was aroused. To cut a long story short, we saw a lot of each other after that. I later found out that she had been a radar technician in the Royal Air Force during the war. As a present that Christmas, she gave me a radio set which she had built herself from scratch. We were married on 10 June 1948 and now have three sons, Babatunde, Alan Adebayo and Oladele.

About six months after I had gone down from Cambridge, I left No 30B, Lexham Gardens for Nutford House, a Colonial Office hostel situated off the Edgware Road. Among the students at Nutford House

19

at the time, were a few Nigerians. Others were Seretse Khama, who later became President of Botswana; Forbes-Burnham, now the Prime Minister of Guyana; and Kojo Botsio from Brasenose College, Oxford, later to become the Foreign Minister of independent Ghana. Among the Nigerians were Gboyega Ademela; Ola Akinkugbe (now in the Federal Court of Appeal); Adi, the late Emir of Wukari; Professor Chike Obi, the mathematician; the late Dape Aderemi; and Alhaji Audu Gusau, who played a large part in the public life of Nigeria immediately after Independence up to the time of the first coup. We were all hand-picked by the Colonial Office as 'good boys', but unknown to them, we all still met and plotted against the 'wicked' British! We talked day and night about how to achieve independence for our respective countries and the role each of us would play in sustaining that independence once it has been achieved.

On 14 June 1948, I sailed for home from Dover on a cargo boat, a fully qualified lawyer itching to play my part in Nigeria's postwar reconstruction. Irene stayed behind to learn Yoruba at the School of African and Oriental Studies of the University of London, where she had enrolled a few days after my departure. She joined me in Nigeria six months later.

3 Home again

Living in Nigeria in those days with an English wife was far from normal. The attitude of the British resident in Nigeria at the time to the average Nigerian was very much that of a benevolent colonial master. Open acts of discrimination were quite common. For example, one Sunday, not long after our first son was born in 1951 we took him in a canoe to Tarkwa Bay for the day. We were sitting on the beach when it started raining. As the downpour was rather heavy, we ran into the army officers' mess for shelter. A white army major came out from nowhere and ordered us to leave the premises as it was army property. I explained to him that we had no intention of staying but that we were only sheltering from the rain. He nevertheless ordered us to leave. I was going to argue with him but Irene told me not to and that we should leave. She said she knew the major and that we could lodge a complaint later. She observed, quite rightly, that if anything happened it would be my word against his and nobody would be likely to believe me. We let the officers' mess and went back with 'Tunde into the heavy rain. On our return to Lagos, I made an official report of the incident. The major was directed by the Chief Secretary to the Government (Sir High Foot, later Lord Caradon) to apologise for his conduct in writing, which he did. The prompt action taken on my complaint was not unconnected with my work as Crown Counsel in the Attorney-General's Department at the time.

Irene worked very hard at this time. Apart from her normal day's work she wrote letters to the BBC about events in Nigeria which were broadcast in London. She also represented a number of English newspapers. In addition, she gave a news review once a week on the Nigerian radio entitled 'This Week in Nigeria'. This was a review of the week's events. She also started, almost single-handedly, woman's athletics in Nigeria. Nobody took the girls seriously at first. Irene persisted, nevertheless, spending her own money in organising the sport.

On my arrival in Lagos, I was enrolled as a barrister and solicitor of the Supreme Court of Nigeria. For a time, I was in chambers with Remi Fani-Kayode and Rotimi Williams. Later I acquired my own set of chambers at No 14, Bankole Street, Lagos. Among the judges before whom I appeared early in my career in Lagos, was Sir Adetokunbo Ademola. He then sat as a new puisne judge in the Supreme Court (now the High Court) in Tinubu Square. Later I worked for him as his Chief Registrar for a short period in Ibadan when he was the Chief Justice of the Western Region. Much later, I became a colleague of his in the Supreme Court when he was Chief Justice of Nigeria. Sir Adetokunbo Ademola was a kind, courteous, humane judge; his displeasure could be quickly stirred against those who had deliberately flouted the law or who wilfully caused unnecessary suffering to others.

My first murder case was a nightmare. Some time in June 1949, I was briefed by the Senior Registrar of the Supreme Court to appear for the defence in the case. It was what we called in those days a 'Crown brief'. The pay for the work was poor but it afforded one an opportunity to gain some necessary experience in advocacy. Mr Dennis Stephens, a Crown Counsel in the Attorney-General's Department, appeared for the prosecution.

The accused was a Northerner from Gusau who was

charged with the murder of one of the occupiers of the house which he was alleged to have broken into near Sabo in Ebute Metta. The case for the prosecution, put shortly, was that he stabbed the deceased, who was one of those who pursued him after he had been apprehended. Before the trial, I went, after reading the record of the preliminary investigation before the magistrate, to see the accused in the prison at Broad Street, Lagos, where he was in custody. I noticed that he had matchet cuts and bruises, which had since healed, all over his body. I asked him how he came by them. He replied that his pursuers on the night in question had attacked him with knives and matchets. I asked whether this was before he stabbed the deceased or after. He denied stabbing the deceased although there was evidence that the knife with which the deceased was stabbed had his finger prints on the handle. I pressed him further about this but he stuck to his denial. He then explained that he was walking home on the night in question when a group of people came out of the house shouting, 'thief, thief' and, on seeing him, mistook him for the thief, gave him many matchet cuts and then arrested him. He stuck to this story, although there was evidence in the preliminary proceedings which showed clearly that he was identified by more than three persons carrying a box full of clothes and trinkets from the premises.

At the jury trial presided over by Mr Justice Gregg, an Englishman, the pathologist repeated his evidence that the knife produced to him in court which had the fingerprints of the accused on it was the one which caused the stab-wound from which the deceased died. Under cross-examination by me, he admitted examining the accused, who had been admitted into hospital a day or two after the burglary, and had found him covered with fresh matchet wounds which could not have been self-inflicted. When I questioned him about the approximate date of the injuries, he admitted that they could have been inflicted on the night of the burglary. The three occupiers of the premises, who also testified for the prosecution, denied emphatically that anybody touched the accused on the night of the incident. They insisted, when I questioned them about the injuries, that all they did was to pursue the accused and after apprehending him handed him over to the policeman who had arrived at the scene later. They were unable to explain how the accused man came to have the matchet cuts. For his part, the accused stuck to the earlier story which he had told me. He denied most vehemently either that he broke into the premises of the complainant's and stole their clothes or that he stabbed the deceased.

The jury, after retiring for about two hours, came back and returned a verdict of guilty of murder. Presumably, because of the version given by the accused in his defence on oath, they completely ignored the element of self-defence which I had urged. The conviction was later confirmed on appeal by the West African Court of Appeal. I must confess that even now, I am still convinced that the accused lied unnecessarily. He could not see the point I urged upon him that he was not being tried for burglary but for murder. I pointed out that there was overwhelming evidence that he committed the burglary and that he might as well admit it. I also pointed out to him that although there was overwhelming evidence that he was the one who stabbed the deceased, the time of the stabbing was not clear. The line of defence I envisaged was this. If the jury could be convinced, firstly, that although the accused might be a thief, he was not a murderer, and, secondly, that he stabbed the deceased in self-defence after he had been savagely attacked by his pursuers, I might succeed in the defence of self-defence. Of course, his complete denial of every allegation, which was patently untrue, knocked the bottom out of my case. For days thereafter I brooded over the conviction. I was convinced that if he had been more candid with the court, I might have got him off the charge of murder. I have spent many sleepless nights wondering whether justice was actually done!

Another case in which I appeared for the defence, was that of *The King v Emmanuel Oyefolu & Others*. The five accused persons were charged with breaking into the shop of the British West Africa Corporation (BEWAC) along the Marina in Lagos, and stealing the sum of about £8,000 from the safe. The case for the prosecution was based mainly on access to the keys of the shop and to one of the keys to the safe, both of which were kept by the chief accountant, an expatriate who lived in a flat nearby. The first accused – Emmanuel Oyefolu – was the chief accountant's steward. The second accused was the cashier who kept the other key of the safe. Neither the chief accountant nor the cashier could open the safe without the other being present and surrendering his own key. Another accused was the messenger who locked up the shop at closing time each day.

The case against the accused persons was that the cashier conspired with both the messenger and the chief accountant's steward who helped him to procure the other keys from the chief accountant's flat, opened the safe quickly with the keys, removed the money, locked the safe again and returned the keys to the dressing-table from where they had been taken. The chief accountant, in his testimony before the court, con-firmed that it was his habit, every day after work, to return to his flat, empty the contents of his pocket, which included all the office keys, on to his dressing table and go into his bathroom for a shave and a bath. After his bath, he would change and then collect all the keys again and put them in his pocket. He also pointed out that he usually spent between ten and fifteen minutes in the bath.

In the course of the trial, which was presided over by Mr Justice Adetokunbo Ademola, an application was made by one of the defence counsel that the court should visit both the flat and the shop. This was in order to determine how valid was the contention of the prosecution that the steward, who was my client, had had the opportunity to take the chief accountant's keys, open the safe, and return them before he (the chief accountant) came out of the bathroom. Unfortunately, when the court visited the *locus in quo*, my client was not present. Nevertheless, three of the accused persons, including my client, were convicted of the offence charged and sentenced to five years' imprisonment with hard labour.

Immediately after the conviction, I lodged an appeal on the sole ground that the court erred in law in visiting the *locus in quo* in the absence of the steward when the only evidence that connected him with the crime was the fact that he had an opportunity to remove the key of the safe which was in the custody of the chief account-ant. By the time the appeal was heard, however, I had accepted an appointment as a Crown Counsel in the Attorney-General's Department. I, therefore, passed the brief to the late Samuel Akintola, who later achieved high political office as the Premier of Western Nigeria. Not surprisingly, he argued the appeal successfully. The judgment became the leading case on the procedure to be adopted when a court is visiting the *locus in quo*.

Sir Gerald Howe, later Chief Justice of Hong Kong, was the Attorney-General of Nigeria in 1950. Arthur Riedhart was the Solicitor-General. They both en-couraged me to apply for appointment in the Colonial Legal Service as a Crown Counsel. After much hesita-tion, mainly because my practice at the Bar had started to expand, I made the necessary application. After the usual interview, I was duly appointed a Crown Counsel in October 1950. At the time, there were very few Nigerians in the professional cadre of the Legal Depart-ment. For years, the only Nigerian was the late Richard Doherty, who was later appointed the first Speaker of the Western House of Assembly. He retired from the public service as a judge of the High Court of Western Nigeria. Other Nigerians appointed as Crown Counsel around the same time as myself were the late Ernest Egbuna (later Speaker of the Eastern House of Assembly); Godfrey Amachree, later Solicitor-General of the Federation and at one time one of the Assistants to the United Nations Secretary-General; Basil Adedipe, later Mr Justice Adedipe of the High Court of Lagos; and Mr Charles Madarikan, later Mr Justice Madarikan of the Supreme Court of Nigeria. All the other legal officers, about eleven in all, were expatriates. I was very happy in the Legal Department. The relationship, both official and social, among all the professional officers in the department could not have been better, with mutual respect and confidence all round.

In November 1950, I moved into No 5, Cameron Road, Ikoyi, the first Government quarters I was to occupy. Opposite me was the late Mr Edmund Otun, then a young dentist in the Medical Department. Close by was Mr Ben Enwonwu, the celebrated Nigerian artist, in the process of making an international reputation for himself. Each of us occupied a one-bedroomed storey-house in Cameron Road. Each house was like a square box in a large garden and, because of this, the houses were then popularly referred to as 'signal boxes'. There were very few Nigerians living in Ikoyi at the time. I recall the names of Dr Oladele Ajose, later Professor Ajose; Dr Manuwa, later Sir Samuel Manuwa; Mr Justice O Jibowu, later Sir Olumuyiwa Jibowu; Dr Adekoye Majekodunmi, then a specialist in the Massey Street dispensary. As a matter of fact, Ikoyi and other Government reservation areas all over the country, known earlier as European quarters, were not opened up to Nigerians until about 1945 after what was generally known as 'the Bristol Hotel incident', which came about when a Colonial Office official, a mulatto, – was refused accommodation at the Bristol Hotel in Martin Street while his white boss was given accommodation. A number of former Nigerian students who had then returned home, led by Prince Adeleke Adedoyin, a lawyer, who was then a prominent member of the National Council of Nigeria and the Cameroons (NCNC), protested about the treatment so vehemently that the Government of the day, under the able and determined governorship of Sir Arthur Richards, later Lord Milverton, decided that all public places such as hotels, hospitals and rest-houses, should be open to Nigerians and all coloured persons who could afford to pay for the accommodation and facilities provided. It was as a follow-up to this decision that what used to be regarded then as European quarters were made available to Nigerians who were then in the senior service of the Government. Even so, the clubs all over the country which were still considered as private and inviolate were not thrown open to Nigerians until 1953. I will have more to say about this later.

No 5, Cameron Road brought back memories of my boyhood days when we used to leave the 'native quarters in central Lagos and go to Ikoyi in the afternoon to look for cashews during the harmattan season. I remember that one day we went to Ikoyi to look for cashews. The trees were usually in the gardens of the houses located there and we always made sure that the houses were unoccupied before going into the gardens. On this occasion, we spotted what appeared to us to be an unoccupied house along Bedwell Road. We entered the compound. As I was rather small and agile at the time, I was the one who climbed up the tree. I went up and started shaking the branches of the tree so that the ripe cashew fruits started dropping by the score. All of a sudden, and without any notice to me, all my friends took to their heels. Looking round, I saw the occupier of the house, a white man of about six feet two inches tall, coming towards me with a large dog. I stayed up the tree. He moved nearer and asked me to come down. I refused. When he repeated the order, I told him that I would not come down until he had removed his dog. He yelled at me but I stayed put on the tree. I would not budge. My shirt and trousers were still lying on the ground where I had left them when climbing the tree. Meanwhile, my friends had deserted me and had succeeded in taking with them most of the cashew fruits which we had collected and put in a bag as they dropped down. Eventually, seeing my tears, the white man relented and went back into his house with the dog. As the door shut behind him, I jumped down from the tree, picked up my clothes and ran like a sprinter in my underpants. The irony was that fifteen years later I was able to occupy one of those houses with my own cashew trees in the garden!

A few months after I moved into the house in Cameron Road, a car drove into the compound early one evening after the gardener had left. I was walking round checking up on his work for the day. I had on a pair of khaki shorts and a rather tatty shirt. Out of the car came a young Englishman. He must have thought I was the gardener. He said to me in pidgin English, 'Which place No 2, Lugard Avenue de?'. I rose to the occasion and replied in the same vein, 'No 2 de over dia', pointing to the intersection at Second Avenue and Lugard Avenue. He then retorted, 'Make you come out and show me for road'. I duly complied, went to the road with him and said, 'Dis na de place'. Without even thanking me, he jumped into his car and drove off. About a week later I went to a cocktail party in Ikoyi. Also there was this young Englishman. I was talking to another guest who was a friend of mine, when this man, who obviously knew him, walked up to us. After being introduced, the man said to me, 'I am sure I have seen your face somewhere'. I replied, 'You are not far wrong, I was the gardener you spoke to in Cameron Road about a week ago'. While he was rather embarrassed at being reminded of the encounter, I just laughed it off.

Relationships between Nigerians and expatriates were not as cordial then as they are now. We were at that time just beginning to get to know each other socially. Of course, those of us who had been to universities abroad were rather impatient with the superior attitude of some of the expatriates living amongst us. Another thorny point was the fact that we were not allowed to join the Ikoyi Club which was then still regarded as a European club and a bastion of expatriate superiority. All this changed in 1953 when the Governor-General, the late Sir John McPherson, insisted that all the so-called European clubs should open their doors to all Nigerians or face being closed down. The expatriates were surprised that not many Nigerians applied for membership after the clubs had been thrown open. Many of us did not join until much later.

Of the few Nigerian judges in those days, Mr Justice Jibowu, later Sir Olumuyiwa Jibowu, Chief Justice of Western Nigeria, was easily the most brilliant and the most hard-working. Being the first Nigerian ever to be appointed a magistrate, he had to work much harder than his expatriate counterpart, both to justify the experiment and to prove to himself that he was as good if not much better than his expatriate colleagues. An Oxford graduate with a kind heart and deep consideration for the feelings of others, he made us all appreciate the value of hard work in the early days of our career at the Bar. Behind a rather gruff exterior, Sir Olumuyiwa had a sense of humour and charm that had brought him the admiration, respect and affection even of those members of the legal profession who had been foolish enough to try to influence him with a flow of fine but meaningless verbiage. His skill at cutting through the waffle and reaching the heart of the matter in a few carefully selected sentences, had always stood him in good stead. Unfortunately, his promising career was dented by the notorious 'Savage letter'. Apparently, the learned judge wrote a purely personal letter to Savage extolling the virtues of a particular political leader. Unknown to him, this letter fell into the hands of the leader of a rival political party against which he had in the past given judgment. The letter was eventually published in one of the local papers at a crucial point in his judicial career. Because of this letter, which seemed to indicate his partisanship in local politics, he never held the highest judicial office, which he certainly deserved, before he died. Having served under him as his Chief Registrar for about a year before he died in 1959, I was amazed at his dedicated detachment in respect of cases heard by him and I was convinced that the allegations were totally unjustified.

In those halcyon days, the 'giants' at the Bar were Sir Adeyomo Alakija, Alhaji Jibril Martin, Alhaji B A Agusto, E J Alex-Taylor, J I Conrad Taylor (later Mr Justice J I C Taylor), Ladipo Odunsi, Chief Bode Thomas and Chief Oladipo Moore; close behind them were those who may be regarded as my contemporaries – Chief Rotimi Williams, Chief H O Davies, Chief Fani-Kayode, Dr G B A Coker (later Mr Justice Coker), Dr Udo Udoma (later Sir Udo Udoma of the Supreme Court), J T Nelson-Williams, Chike Idigbe (later Mr Justice Idigbe of the Supreme Court), Olajide Alakija (alias 'Square Shoulder') and Mr Justice H U Kaine. Also in evidence were Mr Justice S O Lambo, A O Lawson, Chief S L A Akintola and Chris Ogunbanjo. In the course of my career, I appeared either with or against most of those who were based in Lagos.

My closest friend and colleague at the Bar was Chief Rotimi Williams. When we were in our teens, he was known as 'Tiny Tim' while I was referred to as 'Fatus Est'. Rotimi Williams is great in every sense of the word. Perhaps the finest of his qualities is his loyalty. His friendship and confidence, once given, are lasting and immutable. In the normal ups and downs of life, one becomes accustomed to the fact that there are people who unconsciously act as convenient barometers of one's public image. When one's stock is low, one is conscious of not being altogether welcome. As it rises, so does the warmth of one's reception. Rotimi Williams, to his friends, is as constant as the northern star. As a lawyer, and a very eminent one at that, he is a master of the difficult art of clear, impartial and accurate presentation of a case. He never overstates, although he sometimes exaggerates his case. His lucid mind achieves a quiet, searching cross-examination that is both deadly and penetrating. His knowledge of the law, both civil and criminal, is profound. He is a model of what a counsel arguing an appeal in the highest court in the land ought to be – calm, erudite, and resourceful.

Three years after I had been appointed Crown Counsel, there was a sudden mushrooming of commercial banks in Lagos. In those days, all one had to do to establish a bank was to register the bank as one would register any other limited liability company. It was that easy. No large capital was required nor was there any law as to the bank's liquidity. Because of this, all sorts of indigenous banks, which were really fronts for fraudulent transactions, were established overnight. It fell to my lot, as the Crown Counsel responsible for litigation in Lagos at the time, to prosecute the directors of these fraudulent banks. In this connection, I recall the case of *The King v Emmanuel Aladesuru & three others*. The four accused, three of whom were the directors of the Bank and the fourth the auditor, were charged with the offence of publishing a false statement of account, punishable under section 436 of the Criminal Code. Evidence was adduced at the trial to show that many of the particulars in the audited accounts of the Bank were false and misleading. After a trial which lasted more than six weeks, the three directors were convicted. Their appeals, first to the West African Court of Appeal and later to the Privy Council in London, were dismissed.

As a result of all these cases, the Banking Ordinance,

which regulated the business of banking for the first time in Nigeria, was enacted in 1952 as Ordinance No 15 of 1952.

In June 1951, Irene went to the United Kingdom on holiday. She wanted to see her parents and also to show them our son Tunde who was then just over a year old. While she was away, I was posted temporarily to Enugu on relief duty. My boss there was Geoffrey Briggs, later Sir Geoffrey Briggs, Chief Justice of Hong Kong. He was then a Senior Crown Counsel in charge of the branch of the Legal Department in Enugu. A product of Marlborough and Magdalen College, Oxford, Geoffrey was a cultivated man with a taste for high and expensive living. It was generally accepted that he could afford his expensive tastes. Being a bachelor he was the most eligible single man in Enugu in those days. On my arrival in Enugu, Geoffrey asked me to stay with him for a few days until my own quarters were ready. Shortly thereafter, he left me in his beautiful bungalow and went on tour to Abakaliki. I used his main bedroom where I unpacked a few of my things, leaving photographs of Irene and Tunde, in two separate frames, on his dressing table. Unknown to me, Geoffrey had arranged a drinks party in my honour to coincide with his return from tour. Returning early on the day of the drinks party, he informed me that he would be expecting about fifty guests that evening. At about 6.30 in the evening, the guests started to arrive. They consisted of a cross-section of the official community in Enugu. Many of them were expatriate confidential secretaries, some of them very attractive indeed. Apparently, at some stage during the party, one of the secretaries went into the bedroom to powder her nose. She saw the photograph of Tunde on the dressing table; Irene's had, unknown to me, fallen face downwards on the dressing table. Seeing the photograph of a coloured boy of about a year old, this guest immediately assumed that Geoffrey must have been up to some frolicking while on tour! When she

33

came out of the room, Geoffrey noticed an outbreak of giggling and whispering. The first secretary was soon followed by a succession of young women who had suddenly developed an urge to powder their noses and who made their way into Geoffrey's bedroom ostensibly for that purpose! Geoffrey sensed that something was amiss, and went into his bedroom after the last visitor had emerged. It was then that he noticed what had happened. He seized my wife's photograph, brought it out and, in the course of a short speech welcoming me to Enugu, indicated who Tunde and Irene were. The tension was at once defused amidst hilarious laughter.

About half way during my tour of duty in Enugu, Geoffrey received a telegram from the Superintendent of Police in Buea requesting that a Crown Counsel might be sent to prosecute a case of obtaining a large quantity of goods by false pretences. The Southern Cameroons, of which Buea was then the capital, were part of Nigeria and the Senior Crown Counsel at Enugu handled all their legal matters. Geoffrey asked me if I would like to go. Not having visited the Camaroons before, I agreed with alacrity. With his usual boyish taste for mischief, he sent a telegram back stating –

'Williams, Crown Counsel, will arrive at Buea on Saturday 5th October, 1951.'

He later showed me the copy of the telegram and observed, that he had no doubt that with my name they would be expecting an expatriate Crown Counsel. At that time, Charles Madarikan was the only Nigerian Crown Counsel who had ever been in the East. A few days later, I left Enugu for Calabar in my car. From Calabar, I went by plane – a Dove which could carry only seven passengers – for Buea. I was the only black passenger on the plane. Dressed only in a pair of white shorts and an open-neck shirt, I looked more like somebody's clean steward than a law officer. On our arrival at Buea, I noticed that a small reception committee of expatriate public officers, including the Superintendent of Police, was waiting on the tarmac. I adopted Geoffrey's mischievous stance and just walked past them, noticing as I passed that they were asking each of the remaining six expatriate passengers whether he was Williams, Crown Counsel. Naturally, each of them said he was not. Being aware from the manifest that I must be on the 'plane, the desk clerk was asked to page me. On being asked to come over to the reception desk, I got up from where I was sitting, carried my small suit-case, and walked to the desk. The clerk-in-charge looked up at me and said, with some impatience, 'What do you want?', obviously thinking I was just somebody's cook or steward. I replied, 'I have just been paged'. He then asked, 'What do you mean, you have just been paged?'. I answered, with quiet solemnity, 'I am Williams, Crown Counsel, who has just arrived by 'plane from Calabar'. He looked at me again, and observed with obvious disbelief, 'You, Crown Counsel?' Meanwhile, the Superintendent of Police, having noticed what was happening, walked up to us and asked if I was Mr Williams. I said, 'Yes'. He made his apologies for having failed to recognise me on the plane and called one of his orderlies to collect my suitcase.

On the way from the airport in their station wagon to Victoria, another small town not far away where I was to stay, I was briefed about the case. The accused was the Secretary of the Cameroons Plantation Workers' Union, a union of workers in the vast Cameroons Development Corporation's banana plantation. It appeared that this man had been causing labour troubles on the plantation by making 'impossible' demands on the Corporation. The authorities were determined to put him away for a few years. He was, therefore, charged with obtaining goods from one of the shops provided by the Corporation for its workers by false pretences. Because of the difficulties encountered by the

35

workers in getting to the shops in the town, these shops, where basic provisions such as sugar, cigarettes and milk were sold to them at almost cost-price, were opened at strategic points in the plantation. Apparently, the accused and other workers used to buy provisions from the shops, take them to the town, and sell them to small shopkeepers at an appreciable profit. There is no doubt that the workers were intended to buy the provisions and other goods in the shops only for their own consumption. It was, therefore, false for the Secretary of the Union to pretend that he was buying the goods for his own consumption when, in actual fact, he was re-selling them regularly to shopkeepers in town at a profit. While his action was certain reprehensible, it seemed to me that since there was no 'intent to defraud' the owners of the goods, it could hardly amount to the offence of obtaining the goods by false pretences, although he might have obtained their sale by false pretences.

When I expressed my fears to the Superintendent of Police, he said they would still like the accused to be prosecuted if only to show the others that the action was reprehensible. The trial duly commenced in the Magistrate's Court, Buea, on the following Monday. To my utter surprise, the trial Chief Magistrate, on the above facts, found the accused guilty on each of the three counts under which he had been charged. He was convicted and sentenced to two years imprisonment with hard labour on each count, the sentences to run concurrently. Significantly, the accused did not appeal against the conviction which would certainly have been quashed on appeal. Indeed, justice in the colonial era, particularly in the lower courts, sometimes had many faces!

4 Towards independence

In 1953, a decision was taken to review the McPherson Constitution under which elections had been held throughout the country in the previous year. To this end, a Constitutional Conference was arranged by the British Government to which delegates of the Federal and Regional Governments were invited. Representatives of political parties were also invited. The Conference met in London in 1953 and in Lagos early in 1954.

One of the major decisions taken at the Constitutional Conference was the regionalisation of the judiciary. The Nigerian Bar Association's opposition to the proposal proved abortive since the politicians were bent on controlling the administration of the judiciary of their respective Regions. Apart from the opposition of the Nigerian Bar Association, fears were also expressed in many quarters that the decision might lead to judges and magistrates becoming the tools of politicians. It was also said that the system might eventually lead to the control of the judiciary by the Executive.

Outstanding among those opposed to the regionalisation was Sir John Verity, Chief Justice of Nigeria, 1946–54. After discussing the matter with all his colleagues, Sir John submitted a comprehensive memorandum to the Conference when it resumed sitting in Lagos early in 1954. In it, he ventilated his objections and made counter-proposals. He stressed, albeit without success, the need to remove the judiciary from any form of political control and contended that the only way to make this possible was to see to it that judges of the High Court should enjoy freedom 'from all regional relations'. In a developing country, he said, there was a need to maintain a single standard of learning and professional competence in the administration of justice.

Sir John was so disillusioned with the regionalisation decision that he retired from the Nigerian Judicial Service that same year. A year later, when the Government of the Western Region of Nigeria appointed him Commissioner for Law Revision, I had the opportunity and privilege of working with him as his Deputy, and he talked to me about his fears for the judiciary in Nigeria. His belief that some measure of independence might still be salvaged was sadly misplaced. Without doubt, the control of the judiciary by the Executive contributed in no small measure to the demise of the First Republic. One soon discovered that if a judge was not considered sufficiently reliable or seemed too unpredictable or independent, he was apt to be posted to the least attractive judicial division.

Early in 1955, the Government of the then Western Region of Nigeria, decided to revise the statute laws of the Region. Hitherto, Nigeria, being originally governed by our British colonial masters as a unitary state, had become a true federation after the London Constitutional Conference of 1954. Legislative powers were shared between the Federal Government and the three Regions which formed the federation. Consequently, it became necessary for the Government of the Western Region to extract from the Statute Laws of Nigeria a whole body of statute laws which were considered to be regional in content. Honestly, the exercise, as it turned out to be later, was like unscrambling scrambled eggs! Added to this assignment, was the re-enactment, with suitable modification where necessary, of all English statutes, having force and effect in the Region, which were of general application and in force in Nigeria before 1 January 1900. This was to remove the annoying reference to English statute law when trying to find what the law in Nigeria was in certain matters.

To carry out the assignment, the Government of the Western Region of Nigeria, under the able leadership of Chief Obafemi Awolowo as Premier and Chief Rotimi Williams as Attorney-General, created two posts, those of Commissioner and Assistant Commissioner for Law Revision. I was informed discreetly by the two of them that they would like me to apply for the post of the Assistant Commissioner which was later redesignated as Deputy Commissioner.

Although I was rather flattered by the recognition of my legal competence by two of the most able lawyers in the country at the time, I was, nevertheless, faced with a crisis of decision. I enjoyed my work in the Federal Ministry of Justice. I enjoyed both the intellectual and the social climate there. To transfer to a new Regional Legal Service was like venturing into the unknown. But the challenge was there. After much cogitation, I decided to take the risk and applied for the post. A few weeks later, I had an offer of appointment from the Region's Public Service Commission. Although I had accepted the offer as far back as April 1955, I was not released by Lagos until the following August. It looked as if somebody thought I would change my mind. But I did not.

Unknown to me at the time, Sir John Verity, who by then had retired as Chief Justice, had been approached by Chief Awolowo and Chief Rotimi Williams with a view to persuading him to accept the post of Commissioner for Law Revision and had accepted the invitation. Apparently, one of the conditions was that he should be provided with an able assistant. When my appointment was announced, he wrote me a very nice letter, part of which I proudly reproduce as follows:–

'I was very pleased to hear that you had been appointed to be the Assistant Commissioner for the Law Revision in the Western Region and shall very much look forward to working with you. Had I been consulted I do not think I could have chosen a more congenial colleague or one more likely to be helpful in making a satisfactory start on what will, I think, be a none too easy task'.

Working with Sir John Verity opened up new and demanding opportunities for me in the course of my career. Having been the Chief Justice of Jamaica and Zanzibar before coming to Nigeria as Chief Justice, Sir John had had a long and varied career on the Bench. An Englishman who had been brought up in the West Indies, he was a true Christian and an excellent lawyer who readily shared his long experience with me throughout the three years we worked together. Observant and quietly self-assured, he exercised just the right influence on the work of the Law Revision Commission. Having practised before him for many years in Lagos when he was Chief Justice, I had learnt to admire and respect his erudition. Sir John was easily the most respected of all the judges who sat in the West African Court of Appeal. His judgments, known for their clarity of thought and precision of language, were always eagerly awaited by members of the Bar. To be called upon to work with a person of such calibre was a rare opportunity. One curious fact about Sir John was that he wrote quite legibly with both hands. During the time I worked with him, it was not uncommon for him to write with his right hand for about two weeks and then change to writing with his left hand. Over the years, I was able to tell which hand he was using! When I asked him how he had acquired this facility, he explained that he once broke his right arm as a result of a car accident and because that arm was in a sling for months, he had to learn to write with his left hand so that his work

40

would not suffer. That, in a nutshell, was my superior's attitude to life and work.

The art of government is not to make laws but to know what law to make. The force of this truism was brought home to me in the course of my assignment to the Law Revision Commission. Sir John and I felt it was time that we had an Adoption Law in the Region. We discussed the matter informally with both the Premier, Chief Obafemi Awolowo, and the Attorney-General, Chief Rotimi Williams, who both said they had no objection to a Bill along those lines being prepared. We accordingly drafted an appropriate Bill based on the Adoption Act of the United Kingdom. When the draft Bill was being discussed in the Regional Executive Council, certain members had reservations because they thought the purpose of the Law might be misunderstood by the people of the Region. Nevertheless, the Government accepted the Bill and it was sent to the Government Printer for publication in the Regional Gazette before being debated in the Western House of Assembly. The Opposition members, through one of their most astute politicians, Chief Adegoke Adelabu, then spread the word that the Government of the Western Region of Nigeria was proposing to pass a law which would give them the power to order that your child was no longer yours but belonged to somebody else! This rumour spread like wildfire and was believed throughout the Region. The argument generated was so acrimonious that the Government had to withdraw the Bill. It never saw the light of day again.

Soon after my assumption of duty on the Law Revision Commission, and before Sir John's return to Nigeria, a storm broke out in the Governor's office. At that time the Governor of the Region presided over all Executive Council meetings. When the proposed appointment of the Commissioner for Law Revision was discussed, the Premier and the Minister of Justice, Chief Rotimi Williams, put forward Sir John's name for the post. It then transpired that the Governor, Sir John Rankine, the Attorney-General, Mr Hay, and the Permanent Secretary to the Ministry of Justice and Local Government, Mr R A Brown, had another person in mind. After much discussion, however, the appointment of Sir John Verity was reluctantly agreed upon. The upshot of all this was that, when Sir John eventually arrived in Ibadan, he was made most unwelcome by the moguls of the administrative service. He was given a house normally reserved for cadet administrative officers. Sir John told me that unless something was done to provide him with suitable accommodation he was going back to England on the next available boat. On hearing this, I rushed off to the Minister of Justice and told him of the crisis. He must have discussed the matter with the Premier overnight because the following morning the Premier, Chief Obafemi Awolowo, sent the keys of his own official residence to me with instructions that Sir John Verity could occupy the house for as long as he remained in Nigeria. Funds were also provided, presumably from the vote in the Premier's Office, for the redecoration and the refurnishing of the house. Sir John was so overwhelmed by this show of consideration for his welfare that he observed to me, almost in tears, that while his own people were opposed to his return to Nigeria it was the Nigerians who made him welcome. I could discern the reason for this shabby treatment by officialdom months later in the course of my various and regular discussions with Sir John. Apparently, when he was Chief Justice he had the reputation in official circles of not being sufficiently prepared to bend the demands of justice to suit the whims and caprices of officialdom.

The civil service set-up in the Western Region in those days was rather lopsided. All the permanent secretaries, with the exception of Chief Simeon Adebo, who had just been appointed the Permanent Secretary in the Ministry of Finance, were expatriates. Even in my own comparatively lowly capacity as the Deputy Commissioner for Law Revision, I was one of the most senior Nigerian public officers in the Region at the time. As a result, a situation emerged where all the ministers were Nigerians while all their permanent secretaries were expatriates. Many of these expatriates, quite understandably, wanted things to remain as they were and this was reflected in the advice given by them to their ministers.

Chief Adebo, of course, saw the situation much more clearly than we did. We could only discern what was happening from glimpses at minutes sent down to us from above. Chief Adebo decided that he must do something about the situation. He called a meeting of the most senior Nigerian officers in the Region, both in the public service and in the University of Ibadan. Present at this historic meeting were Chief Adebo, Dr S O Biobaku, Dr Modupe Norman-Williams, Chief I O Dina, M A Bateye, Adeniyi Williams, J O Longe, C O Taiwo, T O Ejiwunmi, A O Shomade, T S Aribisala, Ayo Ogunseye, Zak Odunsi and myself. Chief Adebo explained the situation to us and emphasised the fact that the ministers, who were then new to the intricacies of ministerial government, were not getting the sort of impartial advice which they ought to receive from their expatriate permanent secretaries. Efforts to initiate policies for the benefit of the people of the Region were frustrated if the expatriates did not like them. The inexperienced ministers were almost powerless. After hearing Chief Adebo, we decided to form a club to be known as the 'A' Club after Chief Adebo. Chief Adebo was elected chairman and I was elected secretary. The membership was limited to those present at the meeting, and its purpose was to make the joint experience of the members available to any minister in respect of any matter within his portfolio. All the minister needed to do was to indicate to Chief Adebo that he wanted to attend our next meeting which was held monthly in the house of one of the members.

At that meeting the minister would tell us his

problems and after discussion we would suggest suitable solutions. The ministers were thus able to withstand and overcome the uncooperative attitude of their permanent secretaries and other expatriate officials. The Club, which was established towards the end of 1955, worked secretly but effectively until 1958 when the Western Region attained regional self-government.

With the attainment of regional self-government, most of these expatriates who saw their career prospects in blinkers, collected their 'lump sum compensation' and left the country.

About a year before their exodus, Chief Adebo, who had then become the Head of Service, had arranged for some of the members of the 'A' Club, whose administrative ability he was in a position to vouch for, to be appointed as supernumerary Senior Assistant Secretaries attached to their permanent expatriate counterparts in the various ministries in the Region. Among those so appointed were C O Taiwo for Education, Aribisala for Agriculture, Bateye for the Co-operative department, Ejiwunmi and Longe. Later, Dr S O Biobaku was persuaded to leave his post as the Registrar of the University of Ibadan and take up the appointment of Secretary to the Premier and Executive Council, the first Nigerian to hold the post.

By these manoeuvres, Chief Adebo laid a solid foundation on which the indigenous civil service of the Western Region, which became the envy of the whole Federation, was based. His period in the West was one of dedication, service and sacrifice.

Adebo was a good-natured friendly man, fond of discussion, able to disagree vigorously without rancour. In arguments, he generally sought compromise. But he believed, as I do, that while rules could be flexible, principles are sacrosanct. Towards personal problems he was invariably sympathetic, and in their practical aspects always helpful. He was, as a result, a first-class Head of Service. He never really recovered from the

grave disappointment he suffered at seeing the politicians of the first civilian regime destroy the civil service
edifice which he spent the best years of his life building.

After leaving Western Nigeria, Adebo served first as
Nigeria's Permanent Representative at the United
Nations, later as the Director for Administration under
U Thant and finally, back in Nigeria, as the Chairman
of the National Universities Commission. When the
Constituent Assembly responsible for giving the
country a new constitution was established in 1977, he
was one of the nominated members. As the chairman of
the sub-committee which handled the explosive Federal
Sharia Court of Appeal issue, the compromise which
was agreed to and later approved by the Constituent
Assembly, bore all the marks of his ingenuity. He was a
worthy recipient of the national honour of Commander
of the Federal Republic which the Head of State conferred on him in 1978.

Late in 1956, the Regional Government appointed me
as Sole Commissioner to enquire into the Olukare of
Ikare Chieftaincy dispute. Apparently, the office of the
Olukare of Ikare, a town in Ondo Province not far from
Akure and Owo, had been the subject of protracted and
costly litigation. The various contestants had gone to
court many times over the dispute but the result had
been inconclusive. To settle the matter once and for all,
the Regional Government asked me to make a thorough
investigation into the right of succession to the chieftaincy and to make suitable recommendations.

I duly conducted the inquiry and as a result of my
recommendations, which the Government accepted,
the late Amusa Momoh became the Olukare of Ikare. I
am glad to say that, from that time on, the town of
Ikare has had a period of peace and continuing prosperity.

Early in 1957, the British Government decided to call
another Constitutional Conference in London. Partly
because of my recognised interest in comparative

45

federal constitutions arising out of my work in the Law Revision Commission and partly because I took part in the preparation of some of the memoranda which were later submitted at the Conference, I was appointed as one of the official constitutional advisers to the Western Region delegation. Another constitutional adviser, retained at my suggestion by the Western Nigeria Government, was Sir Ivor Jennings, then Master of Trinity Hall, University of Cambridge, my old college. He was also Downing Professor of the Laws of England. Sir Ivor was a distinguished constitutional lawyer and author of major works on the Cabinet, Parliament, and the history of political parties.

Sir Ivor believed that a constitution is not so much a statement based upon eternal principles as a piece of social engineering designed to meet the circumstances of the moment and to keep the wheels of government turning at least for a short, and preferably, for a long period. He made this clear to our delegation in the advice tendered to us, particularly with respect to the controversial issue of the limited male franchise insisted upon by the Northern delegation for the electorate of Northern Nigeria. It is, indeed, significant that barely twenty-one years later, the vote was given to the women of the North without any objection from anybody.

The Conference, which opened in May 1957, lasted about three weeks. The main topics for discussion were the granting of self-government to the Regions, creation of additional States within the Federation, revision of the franchise including universal adult suffrage, and the regionalisation of the police force. Independence for the entire country was also strongly canvassed by the Nigerian delegation.

Surprisingly enough, the demand for self-government for the Regions which wanted it was readily conceded by the British Government. This agreement went a long way towards granting maximum autonomy in a wide sphere of governmental activities, while at the same time providing safeguards not only against a misuse of power by regional governments, but also against any threat to the functioning of the Federal Government and the continuance of the Federation. Under self-government, regional governors ceased to preside over regional executive council meetings, and lost most of their reserved powers. There were, however, provisions which guaranteed the independence of the judiciary, the civil service, the Audit Department, and the office of the Director of Public Prosecutions.

The Constitution which later emerged also empowered the Governor-General of the Federation, in his discretion and with the approval of the Secretary of State for the Colonies, 'to issue such directions to a Region as might appear to him to be necessary for the purpose of ensuring that the executive authority of the Region was not exercised in such a way as to impede or prejudice the performance of the Federal Government or any of its functions or to endanger the continuance of federal government in Nigeria'.

The joint demand of the various delegations attending the Conference for Independence for the whole country by 1959 was also not seriously opposed by the British Government. Although the Secretary of State re-affirmed his Government's opposition in principle to date-fixing, he, nevertheless, emphasised that his Government stood as firmly behind the objective of full self-government within the Commonwealth as anyone in Nigeria. He proposed that when the Federal elections due to be held in 1959 were complete, the Government leaders, both in Nigeria and in the United Kingdom, 'might confer together to determine the processes by which Nigeria might attain that common objective'. This response did not satisfy the leaders of the Nigerian delegation. After considering the issues left unresolved by the Conference, the delegates decided to shift the final target date from 1959 to 1960. The Secretary of

State was then informed that early in 1960 a new Nigerian Parliament, convened after the Federal elections, would adopt a resolution setting a precise date for independence; they asked him for a more specific commitment on behalf of the British Government.

The Secretary of State promised that upon the receipt of the proposed Resolution, his Government

'would consider it with sympathy and will then be prepared to fix a date when they would accede to the request'.

He further observed that his Government

'would not at this stage give any undertaking that the date would be the same date as asked for in the resolution though we would do our utmost to meet the resolution in a reasonable and practicable manner.'

The following day, the late Sardauna of Sokoto, speaking for the entire Nigerian delegation, made the following statement

'We have given further consideration to the Secretary of State's statement on the independence of the Federation of Nigeria. We feel bound to express our disappointment that it has not been possible for Her Majesty's Government to give an undertaking to grant independence to Nigeria on a date to be named in 1960 by the new Nigerian Parliament.

The year 1959 has been unanimously proposed by the people only because we appreciate that the solution to the various problems that must be disposed of before independence will take longer than we had thought.

Having gone thus far on the path of reason and realism, we had thought that the Secretary of State would accede to our united wishes. In the circumstances, we can do no more than to take note of the Secretary of State's statement, while reserving to

ourselves the right to pursue the issue further with a
view to impressing upon Her Majesty's Government
the necessity for granting independence to the Federation of Nigeria not later than 2nd April, 1960.'

I have no doubt that it was this veiled threat from the
Sardauna which hastened the granting of independence.

At the Conference, the issue of the franchise nearly
resulted in deadlock. The Southern delegation wanted
universal adult suffrage for the whole country during
the coming federal elections while the Northern delegation insisted, on religious grounds, on a limited male
franchise only. Neither delegation would give way. At
one point it looked as if the Conference would have to
break up and return home. Eventually, the matter was
referred to a Committee while the issue of the Nigeria
police was taken up.

The main point of contention vis-à-vis the Police
was this: the Southern delegation wanted the Nigeria
Police to be completely federal in the sense that its
operational control should be in the hands of Federal
Government. The Northern delegation wanted the
Police to be regionalised so that each Region could control the contingent of the Nigeria Police within its bor-
ders. Again, there was deadlock. No solution on this
crucial issue appeared in sight. The matter was therefore
left in abeyance.

A few days later, for some inexplicable reason, each
delegation withdrew its objection to the rigid stand of
the other. One suspected, although I must admit that
there was no clear proof of it, that a lot of horse-trading
went on behind the scenes. That is how the country
came to have a Federal Police Force and a limited male
suffrage lasting more than twenty years for the Northern Region.

A considerable time was also devoted by the Conference to the creation of new States and the problems
of minorities. After a lot of heated arguments with

49

recriminations flying all over the place, it was finally agreed that the problem was of such complexity that it would be best to appoint a Commission of Inquiry to look into it in depth. The Commission was

> 'to ascertain the facts about the fears of minorities in any part of Nigeria and to propose means of allaying those fears whether well or ill-founded.'

However, in order to emphasise its misguided opposition to the breaking up of the country into more States, the British Government stated that it would not consider the creation of more than one new State in each Region, and that even then it would

> 'have to take into account the effect of the establishment of any such new states on the existing Regions in the Federation and on the Federation as a whole . . . and would also have to be satisfied by the Commission that any such new State would be viable from both the economic and administrative points of view, since it was the view of the United Kingdom Government that administrative and other practical reasons would inevitably limit most severely the possibility of the further sub-division of Nigeria into States modelled on the present Regional system.'

The Commission of Inquiry, popularly known as the Minorities Commission under the chairmanship of Sir Henry Willink, Master of Magdalene College, Cambridge, held sittings throughout Nigeria during the latter part of 1957 and early in 1958. Chief Rotimi Williams, T A Bankole-Oki and I appeared for the Government of Western Nigeria during its hearings in Lagos, Ibadan, Oyo, Benin City, Warri, Ilorin, Enugu and Calabar. In accordance with our briefs, we pressed hard for the creation of more States in the country, pointing out, with supporting evidence, that the Federation as it was then was too lopsided. We also emphasised the fact that the present three Regions, being so strong, powerful and rich, were a threat to the corporate existence of the Federation. All our pleas fell on deaf ears. At one of the sittings, I think it was in Benin City, we got so fed up at being blatantly ignored and ridiculed by the members of the Commission, that we decided, with the approval of the Premier (Chief Awolowo), to withdraw from further proceedings of the Commission. It took some time before we were persuaded to go back.

Even though we returned, we had no doubt in our minds, partly because of the subtle caveat entered by the British Government in the Commission's terms of reference, and partly because of the impatient attitude of the members of the Commission to our case, that they would make no recommendations for the creation of any more States in the Federation.

We were, therefore, not surprised at the Commission's Report which came out later in the year. Although the members of the Commission did say in their report that they found the existence of genuine fears on the part of minorities they did not think that the creation of more States in the Federation the best means of allaying those fears. Instead, they recommended a series of ineffective palliatives. One wonders whether, if the Minorities Commission had recommended the creation of more States in the country, the stress which the Federation later found unbearable and resulted first in rigged elections, later in the final collapse of the First Republic, and finally in the military takeover and the civil war would have appeared at all.

After the completion of my assignment before the Minorities Commission and the completion of my work with the Law Revision Commission, I was appointed the Chief Registrar of the High Court of the Western Region in March 1958.

In 1957, after the Nigerian Constitutional Conference, I travelled under an exchange programme to the United States of America. The visit was arranged for me by the United States Information Service in Ibadan and I was a guest of the American Government throughout my stay. The visit was to enable me to study at first-hand the workings of a federal system of government. The visit was replete with excitement for me. I was feverishly curious about the United States and gazed in wonder at every new town, at the broad asphalted highways, at the American farmers in their fields, at the bureaucrats in their offices. I was touched by the easy way in which men and women started conversation, asking and answering questions with a childish frankness and, sometimes, naivety. From some of the books I had read, I was prepared for the abject poverty I saw in the black ghettoes. The deep bitterness and resentment which surfaced later in the sixties had then not erupted. But even then it was apparent. I discerned it every time I talked to a black, whether in New York, Washington, Chicago, Houston or Miami. Without exception, the blacks advised me not to allow myself to be brainwashed by stage-managed government hospitality.

Within a few weeks of my arrival in the United States, I came to know that America had its own share of misery and injustice. The black demand for integration and equal job opportunities which came later was, therefore, not unexpected. Neither was the violence which accompanied it. It was the result of the resentment which had been bottled up by the blacks for centuries.

One of the highlights of my visit was a meeting with Justice Felix Frankfurter of the Supreme Court. A small frail man, he was the Dean of Harvard Law School before his nomination for the Supreme Court by President Roosevelt. Although expected to be one of the progressive members of the Court, he turned out to be one of the most conservative. President Roosevelt never forgave him for this. He was certainly a most controversial figure in the Washington of those days. I spent two unforgettable hours with Justice Frankfurter. With his agile brain and his vast knowledge of how federalism worked, he answered all my questions clearly and simply, much better than in any literature on the subject. During the course of our discussion, he produced a copy of the Western Region of Nigeria Law Reports which I was then editing in Ibadan. He discussed some of the judgments which had been reported. I was quite aware that this was no spontaneous action on his part but that he did it all just to show me that he was also interested in some of my work. Coming from such a great and busy man, it was a gesture which I appreciated immensely. The experience I gained in the United States was most rewarding. I was able to draw upon it for many years afterwards.

After spending six weeks in the United States, I went over to Canada for two weeks where I joined Mike De Winton our Solicitor-General. We toured Canada together, talking to both Federal and State functionaries. It struck us that in the quasi-federal set-up, wherever the Minister was English-speaking, the deputy Minister was French-speaking. If the Minister was French-speaking, the deputy Minister was English-speaking. Being aware of our many-sided ethnic problems back in Nigeria, we thought how easy it seemed for Canada to solve hers. Of course, we did not realise at the time that the problem would defy that simple solution!

On our return to Nigeria, De Winton and I submitted a joint report to Chief Rotimi Williams, the Attorney-General. The reorganisation of the Ministry of Justice in Ibadan, following the grant of internal self-government to Western Nigeria, was based mainly on this report. The reforms were followed first by the other two Regions and later by the Federal Ministry of Justice.

5 Western Region

I assumed duty as Chief Registrar in Ibadan on 1 May 1958. Not long after, I was directed to take on the duties of the Secretary to the Judicial Service Commission of the Region. This Commission was, from 1954, responsible for the appointment and promotion of all judicial officers such as High Court judges, magistrates and registrars. It was also responsible for exercising disciplinary control over judicial officers. On taking over the duties of the Secretary to the Judicial Service Commission, all the files were forwarded to me from the Governor's Office. You can imagine my shock and disillusionment when, on going through the files, I discovered that Sir John Rankine, the Governor of the Western Region at the time, had opposed my appointment on three consecutive occasions, not on the ground that I was unsuitable or unqualified, but on the ground that, at the age of forty, I was too young for the post. Fortunately for me, the Commission stuck to its decision and eventually the Governor had to approve my appointment.

In order to keep the records of both the Judicial Department and the Judicial Service Commission separate and distinct, I found myself in the curious position of writing a letter in one capacity to myself in another capacity. For example, I would write, as the Chief Registrar, under the direction of the Chief Justice, to the Secretary of the Judicial Service Commission recommending the promotion of a particular magistrate and asking that the recommendation together with all the relevant papers should be placed before the Commission at its next meeting. After the promotion had been considered and approved by the Commission at that meeting, I would write, this time as the Secretary of the Commission, to the Chief Registrar conveying to him the decision of the Commission!

I was Chief Registrar from May 1958 until October 1960, except for a short period of about three months in 1958 when I went back to the Ministry of Justice to act as the Region's Director of Public Prosecutions. As Chief Registrar, I worked under Sir Adetokunbo Ademola for a few months before he went to Lagos to assume duty as the Chief Justice of the Federation. His successor was Sir Olumuyiwa Jibowu, a very hard worker, a human dynamo who wanted everything 'yesterday'. He nearly gave me an ulcer during the year in which he held this exalted office! We became quite close when, in addition to my administrative duties which I thoroughly enjoyed, I offered to do research for him in respect of cases heard by him in court. He accepted the offer with disguised relief. This additional responsibility not only kept me abreast of the law but it also kept me close to Sir Olumuyiwa who originally did not take kindly to my appointment by Sir Adetokunbo Ademola before his own arrival to assume duty as Chief Justice in Ibadan.

Sir Olumuyiwa died in May 1959 and was succeeded by Dr R Y Hedges, an Englishman, who had been a judge of the High Court of the Region since 1955. A quiet intellectual with a passion for fishing, Dr Hedges had the knack of making the most involved and complicated legal issues simple and understandable. He never used a word of two syllables when one of one syllable would do. His summary of the facts of a case being tried by him was a model of clarity and I learnt a lot from him. He carried to the Bench a quality of mind, temperament and conduct that made him an admirable judge. No litigant or counsel, whether victor or van-

55

quished, left his court without feeling that Dr Hedges had dealt with the case with impeccable patience and courtesy. But Dr Hedges did not like administration. When he was not sitting in court he was off to Ife, the town in the Western Region famous all over the world for its masks, bronze heads, and carvings, to fish in the nearby Owenna River. As a result, I bore the brunt of the administration of the judicial department during his short tenure of office.

On the retirement of Dr Hedges, Sir Samuel Quashi-Idun, a Ghanaian, who had been appointed earlier as a judge in the Region after he had been summarily dismissed from the Ghana High Court Bench by President Kwame Nkrumah with whom he was in dispute over a case with political overtones, was appointed Chief Justice. A short, thick-set man with a flair for making all those who came into contact with him feel immediately at ease, Sir Samuel was both a good lawyer and a good mixer who enjoyed his work, his whisky and his golf. He was grateful to the Government of the Western Region of Nigeria for giving him the opportunity to continue a career which had been cut short by President Nkrumah's arrogant attitude to the exercise of power. This feeling of gratitude eventually got him into serious trouble with the same Government which had appointed him. He left the Region in 1964 under something of a social cloud.

Not long after Dr Hedges had taken over as Chief Justice of the Western Region in 1959, a note came to him from the Federal Chief Justice asking whether I would wish to be considered for the post of the Chief Registrar of the Supreme Court. I reluctantly agreed that my name should go forward, hoping, however, that the appointment would go to someone in Lagos. To my surprise and alarm, I was offered the post. Fortunately for me a salary revision for the officers in the Public Service was then imminent and there was every likelihood that my present post would be upgraded. I, therefore, wrote to the Ministry of Establishments in Lagos, through whom the offer was made, asking them to assure me that if the Lagos post was graded lower than the post I was holding in Ibadan, they would follow the normal establishment practice and allow me to keep the salary which I would otherwise be earning in Ibadan. A few days later, an abrupt reply arrived stating that they would do no such thing. At that stage, I found that I had no alternative but to refuse the offer of appointment. I did so and sent a copy of my letter to Sir Adetokunbo Ademola, the Chief Justice of Nigeria.

A few weeks later, a query was sent to me through Dr Hedges asking me to explain how I had got to know about the proposed grading for the post of Chief Registrar of the High Court which was supposed at that time to be secret. There was even talk of my being prosecuted for an offence under the Official Secrets Act. Somebody in Lagos was obviously hopping mad at my refusal to accept the post of Chief Registrar! However, and again fortunately for me, a few days before I wrote the letter in which I had asked for the assurance, the gradings of the various public offices in the Region was considered by the Region's House of Assembly during the debate on the Report and Recommendations of the Salary Review Commission. I think it was the Mbanefo Commission. To that extent the proposed grading was, therefore, no longer secret in the Western Region. I replied to the query accordingly and as a result the matter was allowed to rest. As Chief S Ade Ojo aptly put it to me later, why should somebody try to use such a sledgehammer to crack such a nut! Needless to say, Sir Adetokunbo was very cold to me for many years thereafter. The thaw came much later.

I was appointed a judge of the High Court of the Western Region of Nigeria on 7 October 1960, in the middle of the Independence celebrations. Not having had any substantial judicial experience, I was rather apprehensive. As soon as I started to sit, however, I found that the work suited my temperament admirably. Being of a patient nature, I found myself able to suffer fools – both litigant and counsel – gladly enough.

One of the first cases over which I presided in the High Court in Ibadan, where I was first posted, was the case of *Enahoro v Associated Newspapers of Nigeria Ltd* (printers and publishers of the *Southern Nigeria Defender*, one of the newspapers published by the Zik Group). Chief Anthony Enahoro, then a minister in the Government of the Western Region of Nigeria, had instituted legal proceedings in the Ibadan High Court against Associated Newspapers and S N Iweanya, their editor, claiming £5,000 as damages for libels contained in two issues of the newspaper. The first issue contained a report of the proceedings of the Western House of Assembly and the second was an editorial comment based on the report.

The plaintiff was represented by Chief Rotimi Williams and a senior Crown Counsel (Mr Omo-Eboh, now Justice Omo-Eboh of the Federal Court of Appeal); while the defendant was represented by Chief Babatunde Olowofoyeku. For some inexplicable reason, the claim against Iweanya was discontinued before the trial. In supporting his claim, Chief Enahoro maintained that the two publications were grossly inaccurate and that consequently he was defamed. The defendants set up in their statements of defence, the defence of fair comment and qualified privilege.

After hearing the evidence of both parties, I delivered judgment on 1 December 1960. I held that for the plea of fair comment to succeed, the comment must be based on facts accurately stated; and that since the facts, as stated by the first defendant, were grossly inaccurate, that plea must fail. On the defence of qualified privilege, I found that for it to succeed, the defendant must prove that the report of the parliamentary proceedings was fair and accurate and was published *bone fide* and without malice. I also expressed the view that since the defendant had been reckless and had acted in utter disregard for accuracy, that defence also failed.

Before awarding damages, which I later assessed at £1,000 with costs (a large sum in those days), I took into consideration the fact that in spite of the plaintiff's protests the defendants did not publish a correction. Instead, the paper published an even more vicious attack.

Another interesting case which I tried early in 1961, was that of *Taiwo Aoko v Adeyeye Adeyemi & The Director of Public Prosecutions*. The applicant, Taiwo Aoko, had been convicted and sentenced to pay a fine by a Grade 'D' Customary Court at Ijebu-Ijesha for an alleged offence (to which she had pleaded not guilty) of committing adultery by living with another man without an order of judicial separation. Pursuant to this conviction, Chief Rotimi Williams applied to the High Court on her behalf for an order to quash the conviction and set aside all consequential orders based upon it, and to refund to her all sums which she had paid in compliance with the Customary Court's order.

Chief Williams submitted that as there was no written law which she had violated, her conviction was contrary to the provisions of section 21, subsection (10) of the Constitution of the Federation 1960, which stated that no person shall be convicted of a criminal offence unless that offence is defined and the penalty therefore is prescribed in a written law. The application could not be opposed and was not opposed by the two respondents.

After considering the arguments, I held that the conviction of Aoko was in violation of her constitutional right as guaranteed by section 21(1) of the Constitution of the Federation of 1960. I also held that in the circumstances, the conviction should be quashed and the fine, as well as the amounts paid by her as compensation and as costs, should be refunded to her. This decision, straightforward as it seemed became the authority for the proposition that no person in Nigeria can be convicted of any criminal offence not defined in a written law.

In a rather unusual case which I heard later that same year, providence took a hand. In that case, the accused was charged with the offence of being in possession of a plate for printing forged bank notes and also of being in possession of forged currency notes. At the trial the complainant, as the principal witness for the prosecution, had testified that the accused had given him currency notes which he, the complainant, had later found to be forged. He then made a report to the police. The police officer who conducted the investigation into the complaint had testified that when they searched the house of the accused, based on the information which they had earlier received, they found the plate and currency notes in the room of the accused. This witness also testified that the accused told him that he knew nothing about the plate and the notes and that they must have been planted in his room without his knowledge by somebody who wanted to get him into trouble. I noticed that the complainant, in the course of his testimony, was rather fidgety and would not look me in the face.

Some time after the trial had started, the face of the complainant suddenly seemed familiar. I therefore asked him whether I had not seen him somewhere. He murmured something under his breath. I asked him the same question again. He replied, 'Yes, Sir'. Sensing that he had something to hide, I asked, 'Now, tell me where and under what circumstances we have met before'. By this time, he had started to tremble in the witness box. I demanded that he answer my question. To my utter amazement, he replied that when I was a Crown Counsel in Lagos some years before, I had prosecuted him for an offence in the High Court. I asked him to tell the court the offence. He replied that he had been charged with being in possession of forged currency notes. He also admitted, in answer to a final question put to him by the prosecuting State Counsel, who had by then continued his examination-in-chief, that he had been convicted of the offence and sentenced to prison. It is needless to say that after this, the State Counsel felt that the chances of getting a conviction were nil. He therefore decided to offer no further evidence and I found the accused not guilty of the offences charged and acquitted and discharged him. I have never forgotten this case. Since no other judge but I could have known anything about the criminal record of the complainant, I was convinced that Allah in His mysterious way, had purposely intervened during the trial to jolt my memory and thereby see that justice was done.

Not long after the hearing of this case, in June 1961, I went on Holy Pilgrimage to Mecca, partly to give thanks to Allah for my appointment to the High Court Bench and partly in fulfilment of a promise which I made to my father in 1947 when he came to London and asked me to come on the pilgrimage with him. I was unable to accompany him then because I was studying for my final Bar Examinations.

Every Muslim, such as myself, who is capable of undertaking the pilgrimage to Mecca, is obliged to make the journey at least once in a lifetime.

In June 1961, I flew from Lagos to Jeddah to commence the pilgrimage, using part of my annual leave for the purpose. At Jeddah, I stayed in the Kandara Hotel for a few days. While there, I paid a courtesy call on the late Sardauna of Sokoto (the Premier of Northern Nigeria) together with his entourage of about seventy eminent Nigerian pilgrims from the North who were also staying in the hotel. I then flew to Medina for the Friday Prayer. There, near the centre of the city, stands the huge Prophet's Mosque where I prayed with thousands of other pilgrims. This Mosque contains the tombs of the Holy Prophet Mohammed and martyrs such as Abu Bakr and the Caliph Omar. A drape of dark green silk enshrouds the tombs. Above the chamber is the Green Dome. It was here that the Holy Prophet died at the age of sixty-two in 682 AD.

Although a visit to Medina is not really part of the pilgrimage, I flew there for the Friday Prayer because of its many sites of historical interest. These include the unique Qiblatain Mosque where the Prophet relayed Allah's command that the believers, when saying their prayers, should face the Kaabah in Mecca and not Jerusalem. Not far away is the Al-Ahzab Mosque built on the site of the defensive trench which the Muslims dug to fight off the pagans from Mecca. Between the huge Prophet's Mosque and the centre of the city, stands the Mosque of Al-Jumah, where the Holy Prophet offered the first Friday Prayer. Three miles from the town stand the hills of Uhud, where Sayyed Hamzat, the Holy Prophet's uncle, and other Muslim heroes died in battle against the heathens. It was in Medina that the Holy Prophet assembled the large community of Muslim believers which formed the foundation of the first Islamic State.

I flew back to Jeddah the day after the Friday Prayer at Medina. At Jeddah I changed from my Nigerian clothes to the Ihram – the two pieces of white sheet which all male pilgrims wear, one piece worn as a wrapper, the other as a toga. This humble garb signifies that whatever their station in life, all Muslims are equal in the eyes of Allah. Bare-headed and wearing sandals, I then proceeded by car to the Haram, the sacred area about sixty miles from Jeddah, measuring roughly twenty miles long and six miles wide, where all the essential rites of the pilgrimage take place. Only Muslims may enter this sanctuary which contains the city of Mecca, the centres of Mina and Mustalifah, the Plain of Arafat and the Mount of Mercy. Each of these places has a special significance in Islam.

The first place I visited was the city of Mecca, the Sacred City where the Holy Prophet was born and had his first revelation. Mecca houses the Sacred Mosque and its centrepiece, the Kaabah. In 1961, the population of Mecca was about 250,000 but during the pilgrimage, the number swelled to more than two million. One building which dominates all others in this Holy City is the Sacred Mosque which is big enough to hold 500,000 people at a time. In the centre of the great courtyard of the Mosque stands the Kaabah, the first House of God, draped in the black and gold tapestry of the Kiswah. Along with about two million other pilgrims, swarming in and around the Mosque, we formed a sea of white-robed figures which flooded every street, alleyway, and doorway in a spectacular act of piety and devotion. It was a memorable sight which forcibly brought home to me the futility of ambition, of power, and of life itself.

After booking myself into a small hotel nearby, I went to the Great Mosque to pray. With hundreds of other pilgrims, I circled around the Kaabah seven times, performing the Tawaf. I then touched the Black Stone which the Prophet Abraham built into the corner of the Kaabach. I also journeyed seven times to and from the hills of Al-Safa and Al-Marwa as did Hajarat Abraham's wife, in her search for water. Thereafter, I joined other pilgrims in drinking the pure waters of the Well of Zamzam, the well which the Angel Gabriel uncovered when he came to the assistance of Hajarat and her son Ismael.

Vast numbers of pilgrims crowded inside and outside the Great Mosque every time we were called to prayer. During prayers all traffic stopped, business ceased, and everything came to a standstill.

On the ninth day of the pilgrimage, we all poured out of Mecca on foot, on donkeys, on camels, in buses and cars, heading for the plain of Arafat. A whole variety of peoples – Oriental, Negroid, and Caucasian and all the blends brought by generations of intermarriage – were in evidence. I went in a car with Alhaji Busari Obisesan, Alhaji Momoh, Dr Jinadu and Dr Attah, all from

Nigeria. At dusk, we arrived at Mustalifah where we all slept in the open before continuing to Muna at dawn the following day. From Muna we proceeded to Arafat. The day of the Pilgrims at the plain of Arafat will forever remain in my memory. I remember Arafat as an enormous tented city, providing all the services that a city of two million people might need. The whole area was covered with a moving white carpet of humanity, all looking pious, dedicated, eager, and very happy. After much pushing and shoving, I found my way to a place not far from the top of Mount Arafat (the Mount of Mercy) where I prayed and listened to a sermon preached by a local dignitary.

After the visit to Mount Arafat, we all turned and walked back to Mustalifah. The tents having all been taken down and cleared away, the plain of Arafat became once more an empty, rock-covered piece of dusty desert. At Mustalifah, we rested and gathered small stones in preparation for the next ritual at Muna the following day when we used the stones for the ritual stoning of the three obelisks which represent the devil. The ritual is, in fact, a symbolic rejection of the devil and all he stands for.

Having stoned the devil, we bathed and shaved our heads, took off the Ihram and put on our normal clothes as a prelude to the Greater Beiram Festival, when those of us who could afford it slaughtered a sheep, goat or camel in sacrifice to Allah. Part of the meat was cooked and eaten, the rest we gave to the poor. This sacrifice has several meanings. As one writer has put it –

'It commemorates Abraham's willingness to sacrifice his son; it symbolises the believers' readiness to give up what is dearest to them; it marks the Muslim renunciation of idolatrous sacrifice; it offers thanks to God; and it reminds the pilgrim to share his blessings with those less fortunate.'

It has also been said that this symbolic sacrifice is part of the worldwide Muslim celebration of Id-el-Kabir that unites those performing the Hajj with those elsewhere, as all Muslims celebrate the feast, thus sharing in the elation and piety of those on pilgrimage to Mecca.

I flew back to Nigeria exactly three weeks after arriving at Jeddah Airport for this memorable pilgrimage. In recent times, an increasing number of Nigerians have observed that the present reliance on easy charter flights from Nigeria to Jeddah has devalued and diminished the stature of the pilgrim. To restore the worth, they advocate a return to the ascetic tradition of suffering inconvenience. To my mind, whether a pilgrim spends several years walking from Kano to Mecca or flying from Murtala Muhammed Airport to Jeddah, there is little question that the pilgrimage will provide him with the spiritual climax of his life, as well as a profound appreciation of the unity of Islam.

On resuming duty about three weeks after my return from the pilgrimage, I was posted to Benin City to take over the Benin Judicial Division as the sole judge there. The Judicial Division encompasses the whole of Benin Province starting from Ifon in the west to the Ethiope River in the east, from Auchi and Ubiaja in the north to Asaba in the south. The work load was heavy, intricate and challenging.

On my arrival in Benin City, I sensed a feeling of hostility towards my posting. Although everybody with whom I came into contact was polite enough, there was a distinct coolness in my reception. This, I think, was due, firstly, to the fact that the agitation of the Mid-Westerners for the creation of their own State had then reached fever heat. The people of the area had for years worked for the creation of a new State, to be carved out of the Yoruba dominated Western Region. As a Yoruba myself, and the most senior public officer in the area, I was treated as the leader of an unwanted army of occupation! The courtesy call I paid on the late Oba of Benin was a disaster. After exchanging a few words of greeting, he never spoke another word to me until I left him half an hour later! It will be recalled that the Oba was so dedicated to the cause of a Mid-West State that, in order to concentrate on the struggle, he had resigned his Cabinet post in the Government of the Western Region in 1960. The second reason, was the fact that my predecessor in office, who had been in charge of the Division for a period of five years earlier, had been well liked. Not being a Yoruba, he had identified himself with local aspirations and in fact became the first Chief Justice of the Mid-West Region when it was finally formed in 1963.

However, I took refuge in the heavy work-load and worked as hard as I could to clear the judicial congestion. One of the first things I discovered was that the registrar in charge was the one responsible for fixing cases for the judge to hear, and that new cases were being heard while old ones were neglected. Sensing that there were some unethical manoeuvres going on, I decided that all pending cases should be listed in a three-day call-over, arranged in the order in which proceedings were commenced. The fact that the registrar did not like this move justified my fears and I asked that he should be replaced immediately. Having had a new registrar posted to me, I duly took the call-over, fixed the date for the hearing of the cases and then proceeded to hear them in the order in which they were fixed.

One of the first cases I heard in Benin concerned a police officer who was charged with bribery. His defence, as could be discerned from his statement to the police, was that he was not in the town of Ubiaja on the day when he was alleged to have received a bribe from the complainants there. He also said in his statement that he was on tour with the Assistant Commissioner of Police for the Mid-West in another part of the territory on that particular day. Because of this, Mr Irikefe (later Justice Irikefe of the Supreme Court) who appeared for his defence applied for a subpoena to be issued on the Assistant Commissioner of Police, an expatriate stationed in Sapele. The Assistant Commissioner did not respond to the subpoena. Instead, he sent his staff officer, an assistant superintendent, to give evidence on his behalf. Counsel for the accused, with the support of Mr Candid Johnson (later Justice Ademola Johnson of the Lagos High Court), objected strongly to the way the Assistant Commissioner had ignored the subpoena and applied for a Bench Warrant to issue on the Assistant Commissioner of Police to come to the Court to show cause why he should not be punished for disobeying the order of the Court. After hearing the submission of Mr Irikefe, I went into Chambers to consider my ruling. What would happen if I did issue the Bench Warrant, bearing in mind that the Assistant Commissioner of Police concerned was the most senior police officer in the whole of the Mid-West? What policeman would serve the Warrant, I asked myself? What policeman would arrest him? It would not do if the Warrant was issued but could not be served! In the end, I decided to stall and play for time until the following morning. When I resumed sitting, I indicated that I would rise until the following morning and that if the Assistant Commissioner of Police had not shown up by then, a Bench Warrant would certainly issue. This observation must have been passed on to the Assistant Commissioner because promptly at eight o'clock on the following morning he showed up at the High Court premises in Benin City. Since the Warrant had not been issued, I did not refer to the incident again. I just asked that he should be sworn. He was then examined by Mr Irikefe and duly confirmed everything the accused had said. Needless to say, the accused was found not guilty. The young policeman concerned continued his career and he is now a very senior officer.

One evening, just before Christmas, our eldest son, who was then a boarder at King's College, Lagos, arrived in Benin City by bus with two suitcases; one containing his clothes and the other his books. He was tired after the long journey from Lagos so he took the two cases upstairs without opening either of them, had a bath, and then came downstairs to have dinner with us. As we sat down to eat, the doorbell rang, the steward went to open the door and a man walked in. He told the steward he would like to see me. I left the dining room to talk to him. He asked if I had a son named Babatunde and whether he had just arrived in Benin by bus. I replied, yes. He then asked whether he had a blue suitcase with him. Having seen the case, I said yes to this question as well. He then enquired politely whether he could see the case. I thereupon called on Tunde to bring down his blue case. When the case was brought down, the man opened it with alacrity. To our astonishment, the case was packed full with £1 currency notes, thousands of them. It turned out that our visitor was a police officer, that all the notes were forged and that he was returning to the East from the Central Bank in Lagos where he had taken the money for examination and the issue of a certificate of forgery. Unknown to the police officer, the case in which the notes were being taken back to Enugu was the same type and colour as that in which our son carried his books! When the policeman examined the contents of his case in Benin City he found to his horror that it contained, not money, but books belonging to one Babatunde Fatayi-Williams. On enquiry, he discovered that there was a judge of that name stationed in Benin City. He therefore rushed to my quarters in the hope that my son had got his own case. I shall never forget the look of relief on his face when he found that suitcase in our house that evening! He said nobody would have believed him if he had not found the case and had told his superior officers that he had lost it with all its contents!

The civil cases I heard in the Benin Judicial Division were mostly land matters, very dull and time-consuming. However, because I learnt something about the history of the area from these cases, I found them rewarding. There were also a few claims in tort and for breach of contract. Because politics had become polarised in the Mid-West at the time (most people were committed members of either the NCNC or the Action Group), the majority of the criminal cases involving violence had political overtones. When the complainant and his witnesses belonged to one political party, the accused would invariably belong to the other. Consequently, in most of these criminal cases, the first questions asked by counsel in cross-examination dealt with the political affiliations of the witness.

One such case was that in which seven accused persons whose colleagues had been charged before a Customary Court stormed the court while it was sitting, seized the record book after the judges had run for safety, tore up all the pages and scattered the pieces of paper along the main streets of the town of Uromi. Although there was reason to believe, in the political climate of that time, that the accused had acted as they did because they had, with some justification, lost confidence in the court's sense of justice, I had to convict them of the offence, partly because there was overwhelming evidence that they did invade the court on the day in question, put the judges to flight, and destroyed the court records, but mainly because no court of justice duly established by law should be treated in such a manner. To allow a situation like that to go unchecked would have destroyed the whole basis of the administration of justice, particularly at the grassroots. The accused persons appealed to the Supreme Court against their convictions and sentences but all the appeals were dismissed.

Another criminal case over which I presided was that in which the Onogie of Ewohimi, a staunch NCNC supporter, was charged with murder. Mr Candid Ademola Johnson, then Senior Crown Counsel, appeared for the prosecution while Mr Chuba Ikpeazu appeared for the Onogie. As usual, apart from the police witnesses who conducted the investigation and made the arrest, all the witnesses for the prosecution were members of the Action Group. The prosecution witnesses gave so many different versions of how the accused killed the deceased that I thought it would not be safe to adjourn the proceedings without making sure that the prosecution called all their witnesses and closed their case. With the consent of both sides the court sat until 10 pm when the evidence of the last prosecution witness was taken. On the following day, counsel for the accused made a no-case submission which I upheld in a reserved ruling which I delivered a few days later. On the day of my ruling, there was a crowd of about one thousand milling round the temporary court premises. It was frightening, particularly as it was difficult to know which side the crowd was on! After I had delivered the ruling in which I found the Onogie not guilty, pandemonium broke loose. Drums were produced and a spontaneous demonstration of approval started with dancing and singing all through the town.

On 20 May 1962, we read in the Nigerian newspapers that a serious crisis had developed in the Action Group, the political party then in control of the Government of the Western Region. Sir Samuel Quashie-Idun, the Chief Justice, had since his appointment been very close to the Premier and senior members of his Government. This was understandable because it was this Government which had allowed him to resume his career on the Bench by appointing him first as a High Court judge and later as the Chief Justice of the Region, after he had been dismissed by Kwame Nkrumah.

The facts which led to the crisis in the Western Region may be summarised as follows. The late Chief Akintola, then the Premier of the Region, was deposed by the National Executive of the Party and asked to resign his office as Premier. He refused. Instead, he advised Sir Adesoji Aderemi, the Governor of the Region, to dissolve the Regional Legislature so that the claims of the two factions in the party for majority support among the people could be put to the test in an election. This the Governor refused to do. Chief Akintola then asked the Speaker to convene a meeting of the House of Assembly for the 23 May, to consider a motion for a vote of confidence in his Government. On the 21 May, before the House could meet, the Governor purported to remove Chief Akintola from office. It was at this point in the crisis that the Chief Justice decided to return to Ibadan to make himself available for any advice which the Government might need. I advised him to wait in Benin City, see how the situation developed, and not get involved unless he had to, but he would not accept my advice and returned that same day. Rumour later had it that he saw members of the Government on his return to Ibadan and gave them certain assurances regarding the proceedings which had been commenced in his court by Chief Akintola's faction challenging his removal from office by the Governor.

Be that as it may, the Governor, without waiting for the verdict of the court, proceeded to appoint Alhaji Adegbenro as Premier on that same day, 21 May. Consequently, the meeting of the House of Assembly summoned for the 23 May, ended in uproar; the House was a shambles, and the police had to disperse the members with tear gas. A second attempt to hold a meeting of the House resulted in an even more violent fracas in which every bit of furniture was broken, with missiles flying all over the place, and members jumping out of windows in order to escape injury; nonetheless, some heads were broken and some people stabbed.

There seemed to be no duly constituted Government, and it was hard to see how the public affairs of the Region could be carried out in such an atmosphere. Consequently, on 29 May 1962, the Federal Parliament met and resolved that, in pursuance of section 65 of the Constitution of the Federation, a state of public emergency existed. The Western House of Assembly was suspended and Chief Adekoyo Majekodunmi, one of the Federal Ministers, was appointed sole Administrator for the Region.

Meanwhile, when the action challenging the removal of the Premier by the Governor (Sir Adesoji Aderemi) came up for hearing in Ibadan before the Chief Justice of the Region, the Chief Justice, with the agreement of counsel for both sides, referred two questions for the determination of the Federal Supreme Court under section 108(2) of the Constitution of the Federation. The two questions were –

firstly, whether the Governor can validly exercise the power to remove the Premier from office without prior decision or resolution on the floor of the House of Assembly showing that the Premier no longer commands the support of a majority of the House; and

secondly, whether the Governor could rely on materials or information extraneous to the proceedings of the House in exercising such power.

Presumably because of the assurance which the Chief Justice was alleged to have given there, Chief Akintola's faction resented the decision to refer the matter to the Supreme Court for adjudication. They thought the Chief Justice had the power and indeed the duty to deal with the matter promptly and not, as it were, to pass the buck to the Supreme Court. They also felt, rightly or wrongly, that this delay had aggravated the crisis. The result of this loss of confidence was that Sir Samuel was never really accepted by the Akintola Government again. Happily for Sir Samuel, however, he left the Western Region about two years later to take up an appointment as President of the East African Court of

Appeal. He retired from this post after three years and died in Accra, his hometown in Ghana, not long afterwards.

With respect to the two questions referred to the Federal Supreme Court for determination, the Court, by a majority decision, stated in their answer to the first question that the Governor could not validly exercise the power to remove the Premier from office under section 33(10) of the Constitution of Western Nigeria except in consequence of proceedings on the floor of the House, whether in the form of a vote of no confidence or a defeat on a major measure or of a series of defeats on measures of some importance, showing that the Premier no longer commanded the support of a majority of the members of the House of Assembly. Because of this finding, the court found it unnecessary to answer the second question.

In his dissenting judgment, Sir Lionel Brett answered the first question in the affirmative. With respect to the second question, he said that always assuming good faith, the Constitution of the Western Region did not preclude the Governor from acting on any information which he considered reliable.

On receipt of this answer, the Chief Justice gave judgment for Chief Akintola. He also granted an injunction restraining the Governor from removing Chief Akintola from the office of Premier.

However, a year later the Privy Council reversed this decision and held that the answers to the two questions should have been in the affirmative. By its decision, the Council held, in effect, that Chief Akintola had been validly removed by the Governor from his office as Premier. The Federal Government, dissatisfied with this decision, then approved a retrospective amendment to the Constitution of Western Nigeria passed by the Western Nigeria legislature as the Constitution of Western Nigeria (Amendment) Law 1963 (WR Law No 13 of 1963). By this amendment, deemed to have come into operation on 2 October 1960, the judgment of the Privy Council was rendered ineffective and Chief Akintola was able to retain his office as Premier.

In March 1963, I was posted to Akure to take over the Ondo Judicial Division which comprised the whole of Ondo Province, now Ondo State. The judicial work in this Division was also very heavy. Most of the civil work involved disputes over ownership of land, either between communities or between individuals. The criminal trials were mostly for murder. My impression at the time was that Ondo Province had the highest murder rate in the whole of Western Nigeria. The reason for this, I thought, was not far to seek. Those living in the area are mainly members of farming communities, strongly attached to the land and also to their women. A matchet to the average farmer in the area, both young and old, is almost an everyday item of dress. The people of the area are quick-tempered and easily roused to violence. On the least disagreement, out comes the matchet to settle the dispute once and for all!

In one case of murder over which I presided, the accused, on mere suspicion that his wife had committed adultery with another man, attacked her with a matchet and decapitated her. He then took the head to the nearest police station, confessed to his crime after putting the blood-soaked head on the station counter, and asked that he should be arrested and punished for a crime which to him seemed perfectly justifiable!

One of the decisions which gave me the greatest satisfaction during my time in Akure dealt with an application for an interim injunction pending the determination of a main action which involved a dispute over a timber concession by two timber magnates in the area. The plaintiff had complained in his application that, while the action was pending, the defendant had been felling timber in the disputed area and that if he was allowed to continue, there would be no trees left in the area even if he, the plaintiff, won the case. The defendant, in a long counter-affidavit, denied the allegations and said he had not been near the timber bush since the proceedings started. On the day the motion was heard, learned counsel for the plaintiff insisted that timber was still being felled in the area while counsel for the defendant vigorously denied the allegation. The arguments went backwards and forwards. After some time, it occurred to me that the obvious solution to the matter and one which would surely do justice to both parties, was to visit the timber bush, the survey plan of which had already been filed in court. I then announced that the court would adjourn to the bush. Eyebrows were raised and I was informed by one of the parties that the bush was about eight miles off the main road between Akure and Ado-Ekiti. I thought that this was intended to put me off. I was, therefore, even more determined to visit the site. Driving along the road to Ado-Ekiti, we stopped at a point about half-way along the road between the Akure-Owo Road and Ado Ekiti town. All of us, that is, the parties, counsel, registrar, interpreters, court orderlies, and myself, started a long trek into the bush. After we had walked for about six miles, and just as I was thinking how stupid I was to have decided to visit the bush, we came into a large open space where hundreds of Urhobo workers were felling timber. The whole area was covered with logs of timber. I asked for their headman and had him sworn on the spot. With the consent of both parties, I put questions to him. From his answers, I gathered that he and his fellow workers had been felling timber in the bush for the defendant for the past six weeks. By this time, the defendant was nowhere to be found. His counsel, quite understandably, had no question to put to the witness. The court then returned to Akure where I made the order asked for and appointed a receiver to take charge of the logs and collect the proceeds of any sales pending the determination of the case. Counsel for the defendant informed me that he was not aware of what his client had been up to and I believed him. The sequel to all this was that at the end of the day, the defendant did, in fact, win the case. He need not have done what he did!

The year 1964 brought into the open the disagreement within each of the two southern political parties, the Action Group and the NCNC. While the Northern Peoples Congress (NPC) had remained intact, both the NCNC and the Action Group had broken up into factions. The treasonable felony trials which resulted in the conviction and imprisonment of some members of the Awolowo faction of the Action Group had further deepened the divisions within the party. As for the NCNC, most of its Yoruba members felt that the party was dominated by Easterners and that they were not getting their fair share of party patronage. They, therefore, broke away and formed their own faction. Allegations and counter-allegations were peddled daily. Chief Akintola's faction and the Yoruba section of the NCNC started to flirt with the NPC.

This was the state of affairs when, after my return to Ibadan in 1964, the Federal Parliament was dissolved. In 1963, the 1960 Constitution had been replaced and Nigeria became a Republic. Under the new Constitution, all appeals to the Privy Council ceased and the Supreme Court became the final court of appeal for Nigeria. For the purpose of the election, the NPC, the Akintola faction of the Action Group, and the breakaway faction of the NCNC joined together to form another party known as Nigerian National Democratic Party (NNDP). The Awolowo faction of the Action Group joined the main NCNC to form the United Progressive Grand Alliance (UPGA). Although the NNDP won the election, the result was strongly contested by the UPGA which complained of large-scale rigging.

The sequel to this complaint was that my court was inundated with election petitions, twelve from un-

successful UPGA candidates and one from an unsuccessful NNPD candidate. The allegations in each of
the UPGA petitions were identical, given in identical
words in the same number of paragraphs. Reading
through them, one got the impression that each
candidate merely adopted a pro-forma petition already
prepared by the party lawyers.

When the petitions were ripe for hearing, Chief
Williams, the counsel for a successful NNDP candidate
(respondent in the first UPGA petition) applied for
particulars of the allegations made against his client.
Although the application was strongly opposed, I
thought it was in the interest of justice to make the
order. The petitioner appealed to the Supreme Court
against this ruling. In compliance with the provisions of
the Electoral Act that election petitions should be given
priority in the courts, I saw to it that the record of proceedings was ready for the Supreme Court within a
week. In three weeks, the Supreme Court heard the
appeal and dismissed it. Mr Ganiyu Agbaje (now Mr
Justice Agbaje of the Federal Court of Appeal), a very
able, upright, resourceful, and highly respected lawyer,
was unable to get the required particulars from the
petitioner for whom he had appeared. He, therefore,
withdrew not only the first petition which was treated
as a test-case, but also the remaining eleven petitions. I
dismissed all of them with substantial costs in favour of
each respondent.

The petition by the unsuccessful NNDP candidate
was heard later and was also dismissed on the ground
that the allegations of election irregularities could not be
substantiated by credible evidence. The end result was
that I was not at all popular with the leaders of the
UPGA. All sorts of disparaging allegations were made
with respect to my impartiality. I was not, however,
unduly worried because I had discovered since my
appointment as a High Court judge that most of the
politicians in Nigeria and, indeed, in other developing

countries pay only lip-service to the independence of the judiciary. A judge is only regarded as independent, fearless and upright as long as he gives judgment in their favour. In Nigeria, familiarity does not breed contempt. It breeds obligation. As a result, people with whom you are friendly expect you to bend the rules to suit their requirements. It pays in the end for a judge, even at the risk of being accused of being a snob or of haughtiness, to be somewhat aloof, not only from the members of the Executive, but also from the political powerbrokers.

What most of those in power in a developing country fail to appreciate is that in so far as courts of law are concerned, there is a wide difference between allegation and proof. Many a time, although the complaint or allegation might be true, the clear proof of it in court is lacking. This may be deliberate in the sense that the witnesses have been got at by the opposite party or it may be due to inexperience on the part of the person briefed to investigate and handle the case. As a rule, the court, particularly in a civil case, does not wish to descend into the area of conflict. It's duty is to hold the scales of justice between the various conflicting interests. Consequently, if proof of the allegations is lacking, the case is thrown out.

Judges in developing countries, to my mind, should always be careful in considering whether to dispense with the basic requirements of the proper administration of justice. They must be sure, no matter how great the pressure, that such dispensation does not involve essential rights. For example, one sometimes hears impatience expressed by government functionaries with the concern which judges and magistrates have for the rights of a person accused of crime, although they are aware that it is provided in our Constitution that every person so accused is presumed innocent until his guilt is proved beyond reasonable doubt. This impatience may be understandable where the crime is an odious one and the guilt of the accused seems plain to all. Offences under the Foreign Exchange (Anti-Sabotage) Decree of 1977 are a case in point. When such a person is found not guilty by the trial judge, it is important for those in power to evaluate what has occurred during the trial in the larger perspective of the rights guaranteed by the Constitution. It must be remembered that implicit in the democratic system of government is the understanding that any person charged with even the most serious crime must be tried by civilised standards of criminal justice. He should not be tried for an offence which was not an offence at the time when the act complained of was committed. The Constitution must never be allowed, by a twisted process of interpretation, to be distorted by expediency; its underlying commitment to justice must never be compromised.

6 Things fall apart

The political crises that had been building up all over the country came to a head in 1965 after the elections to the Western Region House of Assembly. This election was riddled with all sorts of malpractices aggravated by violence from both parties but more particularly from the party in power, the NNDP. But, like most matters of this type in Nigeria, there is always a wide gulf between knowledge at home, or in the village, and proof in court. Eye witnesses could be bought or sold because the ordinary Nigerian in those hectic, unstable days was convinced that every politician was interested solely in material gain and therefore felt that he might as well extract his own share of the political loot.

Knowing this, the candidates of the United Progressive Grand Alliance (UPGA) which lost the election, did not file any election petitions. They simply refused to accept the results of the election or to acknowledge the legitimacy of the government formed by Chief Akintola. Instead, they and their millions of supporters took to the streets of Western Nigeria, threatening, burning, or maiming any member of the Government party they could corner in the bush or in a back-garden.

Life in those days was certainly not safe in the streets of Ibadan, Ife or Ikeja. Operation 'WET-E' (soak in petrol and burn) was in full swing. Cars of known party stalwarts were set ablaze. Unpopular customary court presidents were slaughtered like rams. To those of us charged with the administration of justice, the fear

1. *The house in which Justice Fatayi-Williams was born at No. 19 Bishop Street, Lagos (now Issa Williams Street)*

2. *Maternal grandfather, late Benjamin Abasi (Ship's Chandler)*

3. *Justice Fatayi-Williams's father, the late Alhaji Issa Williams*

4. *Five of the nine members of the Red Club. L. to r. – Chief I. A. S. Adewale, late Magnus Macaulay, Justice Fatayi-Williams, Victor Haffner and the late Adeolu Allen*

5. *Old Boys' Rally, Methodist Boys' High School, Lagos, 1949. L. to r. – A. Akinosho, A. Fatayi-Williams, Bandele Oyediran, the Headmaster of the school, and Chief H. O. Davies*

6. *Fatayi-Williams at Trinity Hall, Cambridge, 1947*

7. *Graduation Day of A. Fatayi-Williams at Cambridge, June 1946, with his cousin Sir Mobolaji Bank-Anthony and his wife Lady Bank-Anthony*

8. *Wedding photograph, Mr & Mrs A. Fatayi-Williams, which took place in London, June 1948*

9. *Mrs Irene Fatayi-Williams*

10. Fatayi-Williams officiating at Athletic Meeting in Lagos 1949. Standing by
     Dr Nnamdi Azikiwe, third from left, is A. Fatayi-Williams

11. The first Ladies Athletics Meeting in Lagos showing Mrs Hope Bunting, the
     President of the Women's Amateur Athletic Association making a speech and
     Mrs Fatayi-Williams arranging the trophies

12. *Fatayi and Irene with*
    Tunde aged two, 1952

13. *The three sons of the*
    Fatayi-Williams, l. to r. –
    Oladele, aged 4 years,
    Babatunde, aged 10 years
    and Alan, aged 8 years

14. Visit to Nigeria of the Colonial Secretary, Oliver Lyttelton (later Lord Chandos).
Front row l. to r. – the Governor, A. Odulana, Oliver Lyttelton, A. Reffell,
A. Steward. Back row l. to r. – J. K. Randle, Name Unknown, Alex Oni,
A. Fatayi-Williams, S. Nottidge, J. K. Agbaje

15. Chief S. O. Adebo, Mrs Morrison and A. Fatayi-Williams at Constitutional
Conference held in London in August/September, 1957

16. *Conference on the Problems of Federalism held in Lagos in March 1960. Sitting in the front row are: 3rd from left, the late Sir Louis Mbanefo, 5th from left, Lord Diplock, Chief F. R. A. Williams, Lord Denning and Sir Adetokunbo Ademola. Fatayi-Williams is in the back row 5th from left between Mike Winton and H. H. Marshall*

17. *Pilgrimage to Mecca 1961. L. to r. – Dr A. Atta, A. Fatayi-Williams and Dr A. Jinadu*

18.   *A. Fatayi-Williams on appointment as High Court Judge in October, 1960*

19.   Opening of Assizes in Benin, 1961

20. *A. Fatayi-Williams and Fani-Kayode in Ibadan, 1965*

21. *Ports Arbitration Tribunal, 1972. L. to r. – the late Louis Edet, A. Fatayi-Williams and Gus Ehren in Calabar*

22. *Irene Fatayi-Williams with Justice G. S. Sowemimo of the Supreme Court and Justice A. Belgore, then Chief Judge of Plateau State*

23. *A. Fatayi-Williams as Supreme Court Justice in ceremonial robes, 1975*

24. *Some Justices at a drinks party in the premises of the former Chief Justice of Nigeria, Sir Darnley Alexander. L. to r. – Justice A. Obaseki of the Supreme Court, Justice A. Belgore, then Chief Judge of Plateau State, Justice A. Fatayi-Williams of the Supreme Court, Sir Darnley Alexander, Justice M. Bello of the Supreme Court, Justice A. Adefarasin, Chief Judge of Lagos State and Justice C. Idigbe of the Supreme Court*

25. *At the International Conference in Manila, Philippines, 1977. L. to r. – President Marcos of the Philippines, Mrs Marcos, Justice Fatayi-Williams, Chief Justice Fred Castro of the Philippines, and a Justice of the Philippines Supreme Court*

26. L. to r. – Chief Justice Fatayi-Williams, Mrs Fatayi-Williams, Lord Widgery
     (formerly Lord Chief Justice of England) and Lady Widgery on a boat cruise around
     Sydney Harbour, Australia, during an International Conference of Appellate Judges
     held in Sydney, Australia in June, 1980. Lord Widgery died a year later in 1981

27. *The Hon. Chief Justice Fatayi-Williams in his Chambers in the Supreme Court, Lagos, December, 1979*

28. *Chief Justice Fatayi-Williams inspecting the Guard of Honour mounted by the Nigeria Police before the opening of the All Nigeria Magistrates' Conference in Ilorin, capital of Kwara State, November, 1980*

that law and order had broken down irretrievably was always present in our thoughts. Notwithstanding all the signs, the Government kept telling the country that all was well and that they were in complete control of the situation. This, of course, was a delusion, the ominous sense of make-believe which precedes a disastrous fall from grace! Everybody felt that something had to happen to arrest the deteriorating situation but nobody was able to say what.

About 3 am on the morning of 15 January 1966, I had a phone call from Mrs Adia Fani-Kayode, the wife of Chief Fani-Kayode, the Deputy Premier of the Western Region of Nigeria. Adia is a first cousin of mine, her mother and my father being brother and sister. Moreover, my father brought her up and we all lived in the family house at Bankole Street when she was a little girl. Since I was her closest and eldest relation in Ibadan at the time, it was therefore quite natural for her to telephone me and tell me her story in between hysterical outbursts.

Adia told me that some 'thugs in army uniform' and armed with automatic weapons had come to their house just before she phoned and had taken the Deputy Premier away. She thought that her husband's life was in danger and asked me to help. I asked if she had reported the incident to the Governor (Chief Fadahunsi), who lived next door to them, and the Premier (Chief Akintola). She said she had telephoned them and that they had promised to ring her back but as they had not done so she decided to report to me. She also expressed fears for her own safety and for that of her children. I told her that I would see what I could do and that she was not to worry.

After I had finished calming Adia down, I telephoned the house of the Commissioner of Police, Mr Odofin-Bello. There was no reply. I got the same result when I phoned Mr Olawaiye, his deputy. I then telephoned Colonel Legima, the Officer Commanding the 4th

81

Battalion of the Nigerian Army based in Ibadan. His wife answered. She was in uncontrolled hysterics. She asked me why everybody was telephoning her husband. She thought something was wrong and wanted to know because as far as she was concerned her husband was in Lagos attending a meeting of army officers. We were to learn later that Colonel Legima was killed in his room in the Ikoyi Hotel in Lagos by the perpetrators of the coup.

After speaking to Mrs Legima, I telephoned Mr T A Bankole-Oki who lived nearby in the New Reservation and who was then the Director of Public Prosecutions for Western Nigeria. While trying to get through to Mr Oki on the telephone, I heard what sounded like the distant firing of automatic weapons. When there was no reply from Bank-Oki's house, I became rather apprehensive. I therefore jumped into my car and drove to his bungalow which was only about three minutes drive away.

Bank-Oki was fast asleep. It took me about five minutes of continuous banging of his door before he woke up. I told him what had happened and expressed my fears both for Fani-Kayode and for Adia and her children. He said the only action we could take was to drive to the Regional Police Headquarters along the main Abeokuta-Ibadan road nearby and ask for help to collect Adia and her children. On our way to the Police Headquarters, we noticed some distance in front of us the backs of two or three lorries and a Land-Rover. The vehicles turned towards Abeokuta. We were later to learn that the lorries contained the soldiers who had gone to the Premier's Lodge and had gunned down the Premier in his garden and that Fani-Kayode, who was still alive, was sitting in his dressing gown between two soldiers in the Land-Rover. He was being taken to Lagos.

When Bank-Oki and I reached the Police Headquarters, we saw Odofin-Bello and Olawaiye there. We

82

told them what had happened. Olawaiye promised to go for Adia and her children. They lived in the Agodi government residential area which is about three miles away on the other side of town near the road to Ife.

Meanwhile, Odofin-Bello said he was not sure whether those who went to Fani-Fayode's house were in fact thugs, particularly as I had said that they were all in army uniforms. As we were discussing this, a policeman ran into the upstairs room in which we were and told us that there had been an exchange of fire between some soldiers and the Premier at the Premier's Lodge, that the Premier had been shot dead, and that his body was lying in a pool of blood in the garden of the Lodge. As he was one of the policemen who had been on guard-duty at the Premier's Lodge, we thought he ought to know what he was talking about. He said he had to run through the gardens of the adjoining houses in order to escape from the cross-fire.

Odofin-Bello then tried to get the Inspector-General of Police in Lagos on the telephone but all the Lagos lines were dead. While we were thinking what to do next, most of the Regional Ministers who were living in the New Reservation, led by Oba Akran, came into the Police Headquarters. They had also heard the news. They appeared to me like a collection of flustered chickens sheltering from a heavy downpour of rain. The fall from arrogant grace appeared total. I almost burst into laughter. They told Odofin-Bello that they had come to the Police for protection although they well knew that if the soldiers were determined to get them, there would be little which the Police could do to protect them against well-armed troops with automatic weapons.

In the meantime, Mr Olawaiye that kind, resourceful, fearless and indefatigable Deputy Commissioner of Police had turned up again with Adia and her children. Because my own house was too close to that of Oba Akran, I arranged for them to be taken to the house of

Adenekan Ademola. 'Nekan is a very good friend of mine and of Chief Fani-Kayode and could be relied upon not to panic but to look after them until other more permanent arrangements had been made for their safety. Having made these arrangements, I then returned to my own quarters and arranged for Irene and our children to go to the Vice-Chancellor's Lodge at the University of Ibadan and stay with the Lambos who are also good friends of ours. Since I had not told her that there had been an army coup, Irene decided to take a short cut through the Commercial Reservation Area and the army barracks in order to get to the Oyo Road, along which the University campus is situated! Luckily for her, all the soldiers were then away from the barracks and she was able to drive safely through their grounds without any interruption. She did not leave, however, until she had taken the legendary English cup of tea!

By eight in the morning of the 15 January the whole of Ibadan was buzzing with the news of the military takeover. Opposition members and their supporters were out in full force burning the houses of government supporters, particularly in the Oke-Ado area. I had a few threatening telephone calls but these did not worry me unduly. This was probably because I seem to have been endowed by nature with an ability to maintain an attitude of calm detachment in a crisis. I remember that after our ship was sunk in mid-Atlantic on the way to the United Kingdom in 1942, I just stood on the shifting deck of the sinking ship humming the tune of 'Tuxedo Junction'!

By mid-day news had come through to us from Lagos that Chief Fani-Kayode had been set free and was safe, although rather shaken. As a matter of fact, I was in 'Nekan Ademola's house when he phoned through to talk to Adia to let her know about his fate. We were all relieved to learn that he was safe, more especially as we had by then heard that both Alhaji Tafawa Balewa, the Prime Minister, and the Sardauna of Sokoto, the

Premier of Northern Nigeria had been killed by the 'Young Turks' who planned the coup.

Not long after I returned to my quarters in the New Reservation in the afternoon both Oba Akran and Mr Kotoye, another of the Regional Ministers, came to me to ask for the whereabouts of Justice Morgan, the Chief Justice. Apparently, they had been looking for him for some hours. They then informed me that they were looking for Morgan so that he could swear-in Oba Akran as the Acting Premier. Their reason for this was that since, as they thought, both the Premier (Akintola) and the Deputy Premier (Fani-Kayode) had been killed, somebody should be appointed as Acting Premier to carry on the Government and, if possible, restore law and order.

I told them, with a touch of malice, that Chief Fani-Kayode was still alive. Shocked, they asked me how I knew. To think that people who had behaved like frightened chickens earlier in the morning should now be making another bid for power offended against my sense of propriety and I made this clear in my brusque replies to their enquiries. After these exchanges, they left. Nothing was said or heard again about anybody acting as Premier. In any case, within a few days, Lieutenant-Colonel Adekunle Fajuyi had been appointed the Military Governor of the Region with full legislative and executive powers.

Earlier on the day of the coup, Adeyinka Morgan, the Regional Chief Justice, had also received threatening telephone calls. Partly because of this and partly because he did not know to which side the twelve or so soldiers guarding his quarters belonged, he could not summon up the courage to leave. The Chief Justice should not be blamed for this. Since his quarters were at the back of the Premier's Lodge, he and his wife 'Kemi must have had a somewhat traumatic experience earlier in the morning. Be that as it may, Bank-Owi and I decided to look him up later in the day. When we arrived we

noticed that the soldiers were still on duty. We also
noticed that the Chief Justice's nerves were on the point
of cracking. One of his brothers who was with him also
noticed this. Between us, therefore, we arranged for
him and his wife to be driven away from the house in
his brother's car. Being the next senior judge to him in
Ibadan, I asked how I could contact him should I want
him for anything. He said he did not know but that he
would prefer to contact me. Matters were left like that.
He used to phone me once a day to ask how things were
in the court. As the court was not sitting during the few
days following the coup, there was not much to report
in any case. I later gathered, after his contact with me
had stopped, that he had left for the United Kingdom
for medical treatment. Although he returned to resume
his duties a few weeks later, he was never quite forgiven
for abandoning his post at that crucial time. He retired
as the Chief Justice of the Region about a year later.

Lieutenant-Colonel Adekunle Fajuyi took over as the
Military Governor of Western Nigeria after the military
takeover. Except for authorising that Justice Kester,
who was only three months senior to me and was then
posted to Ikeja, should act as the Chief Justice of the
Region during Justice Morgan's absence, he did not
interfere with the judiciary. We carried on as usual in
the performance of our duties although the witch-hunt
of all public officers who were thought to have collab-
orated with the Akintola regime soon started. As will be
seen later, I was one of the victims of this witch-hunt.

Three factors seem to have made me powerful
enemies. Firstly, my rise in my chosen career had been
rather too fast for some tastes. For example, Sir Adetokunbo Ademola preferred me to Kester as the Chief
Registrar of the High Court. Secondly, my decisions on
the election petitions which I heard and determined in
1964 did not please some powerful power-brokers.
Thirdly, in preference to Kester, the Chief Justice
(Adeyinka Morgan) recommended that I should act as

Chief Justice of the Region when he went on overseas leave in 1965. However, as nothing could be proved against me, I was left alone to continue my work, although the undercurrent of character-assassination continued unabated.

We experienced another coup in July 1966. In this second coup, the Head of State, Lieutenant-General Aguiyi-Ironsi, and the Military Governor of Western Nigeria, Lieutenant-Colonel Adekunle Fajuyi were killed. Brigadier Adeyinka Adebayo took over as the Military Governor of Western Nigeria. He set in motion the probing of the conduct of Justice Adeyinka Morgan during his time as Chief Justice. Although he was cleared of all the allegations made against him, Brigadier Adebayo (later General Adebayo) asked the Federal Military Government for Morgan's removal from office on the ground that he had lost the confidence of the people of Western Nigeria. Morgan was duly retired and Justice Kester who, for obvious reasons, had not much love for me, took over as Chief Justice. A few years later, Justice Morgan was appointed President of the Court of Appeal in the Gambia and was, therefore, able to resume his already distinguished career on the Bench.

7 Difficult days

One day in March 1967, while going through my list in court, I noticed that the defendant in one of the fresh cases was a certain Alhaji Hajaig. This defendant was one of the pillars of the Lebanese community in Ibadan. When the case was called, it transpired that the defendant had not been served with the writ of summons. Mr Olatawura (now a judge of the Federal Court of Appeal) who was appearing for the plaintiffs, G B Ollivant, thereupon referred me to an application which they had made to the court under Order 23 rules 2 and 3 of the High Court (Civil Procedure) Rules of Western Nigeria for his arrest as an absconding defendant.

Because of the importance of the application, I decided to adjourn it to the following Wednesday to enable the plaintiffs and the bailiff to make further efforts to serve the defendant with the writ of summons. When the case was called again a few days later, the defendant had still not been served. Apparently, although he had business and commercial interests in Lagos and Ibadan, the defendant was at the material time residing permanently in the Lebanon and was in the habit of coming to Nigeria only once a year. The affidavit filed in support of the application indicated that the plaintiffs believed that if he was not treated as an absconding defendant he would escape once again without paying the sum of about £7,000 which he was alleged to owe the plaintiffs in respect of goods sold and delivered to him by the plaintiffs for which he had refused to pay in spite of repeated demands. Nevertheless, I adjourned the case for two more days to allow the plaintiffs to make a final effort to serve the defendant with the writ. When the appointed day came and the defendant had still not been served, I decided to make an order for his arrest.

Unfortunately for the defendant, he was arrested on the following day, which was a Saturday, just as he was about to board a plane for the Lebanon. The police officers who arrested him brought him directly to Ibadan and kept him in custody at the police station. I only heard about this when Mr Okusaga, a member of the Bar, came to me in the house and asked for bail for the defendant. He also indicated that the defendant's people were prepared to furnish security there and then with respect to the amount being claimed by the plaintiffs. I told him that he ought to know that not only could I not make such an order in my house, but it could also not be made without hearing the plaintiffs who had made the application in the first place. I said he would have to wait until Monday morning when, after hearing both parties, I would make whatever order I considered appropriate. He tried his best to persuade me to make the order but I was adamant. At about 5 pm that same day, I had a telephone call from Chief Rotimi Williams who had been approached by the Lebanese community in Ibadan. I explained the situation to him and he told me that what I had just told him was exactly what he had said to his clients. Two hours later, at about 7 pm the telephone rang again. The voice was that of Brigadier Adeyinka Adebayo, the Military Governor. The Governor explained to me that he had before him a Committee of the Ibadan Lebanese Community which, two weeks before, had donated a substantial sum of money for the Troops Comfort Fund which he, the Governor, had launched earlier in the year. The Governor said that this Committee had come to him to intervene for the release of Alhaji Hajaig and that they were prepared to put up immediately as security a sum of money equivalent to the amount being claimed from the Alhaji. I explained to the Governor in detail what my powers were and repeated to him what I had told Mr Okusaga earlier in the day. I finally told him that because of this, I would not be able to do anything for Alhaji Hajaig until the following Monday morning. Although I sensed some frustration in the Governor's tone, I was adamant in my decision to do nothing. The Governor then dropped the receiver and, as far as I was concerned, that was the end of the matter. I heard later from my Registrar that, in actual fact, Alhaji Hajaig did not spend the night in the police cell. Apparently, he was examined later that evening by a doctor who declared him unwell and, as a result, he was admitted to the Jericho Nursing Home where he spent the weekend in a hospital bed. On the Monday morning he appeared in court to answer both to the claim and to the application of Mr Olatawura. After suitable security had been offered, I released him on bail. When the case duly came up for hearing a few days later, it was apparent that Alhaji Hajaig had no defence to the claim whatsoever. All the invoices by which the goods were delivered to him were duly signed by him or by his agents as having received the goods listed. I therefore had no difficulty in giving judgment in favour of the plaintiffs. As far as I am aware, there was no appeal against my decision.

In fairness to the Military Governor, he appeared to have understood the situation as I had explained it to him. Those who should be blamed for putting him in that difficult situation were the members of the Committee of the Lebanese Community in Ibadan who, because of their earlier contribution to the Troops Comfort Fund, wanted to take undue advantage of his gratitude. They tried, albeit unsuccessfully, to persuade the Military Governor to act in a manner which, by any standards, would have been regarded as an intolerable interference with the independence of the judiciary. As far as I am aware, this decision did not affect the cordial relationship which existed between myself and the Governor. The affair indicated, however, how any person in executive authority should not allow himself, even inadvertently, to be persuaded to act in a manner which could be interpreted as an interference with the due process of the law.

In April 1968, the Military Governor set up a committee to advise him about appointments in the judiciary of the Region. This was after the Aburi Accord when, at the insistence of Colonel Ojukwu, the Military Governor of Eastern Nigeria, and by the Constitution (Suspension and Modification) Decree 1967, the Regions again become autonomous in certain specified matters. The effect of some of the provisions of this Decree was that vis à vis all appointments to the State Court of Appeal and the High Court, a military governor could act more or less as he pleased. Approval by the Supreme Military Council was not required. Furthermore, the appointment of a justice representing a region in the Supreme Court was also on the Military Governor's advice.

The Committee I have referred to consisted of Mr Justice Kester, the new Chief Justice of Western Nigeria, as Chairman. Other members were Justice Oyemade, Mr Peter Odumosu, the Secretary to the Military Government, Dr Festus Ajayi, the Attorney-General, and the late Mr J J Marinho, the Chairman of the State's Public Service Commission. At that time, I came next to the Chief Justice in order of seniority. Since Justice Oyemade, who was junior to me, was preferred to me on the committee, I sensed that something not quite favourable to me was afoot.

Early in May 1968, the Western State Court of Appeal was established by Edict. Later that month various judicial appointments were announced including those to the new Court of Appeal. Justice Kester was appointed the President of the Court. Justice O Somolu and Justice C O Madarikan, both of whom were junior to me, were appointed the Chief Justice of Western Nigeria and a Justice of the Supreme Court respectively. Madarikan was appointed to fill the post allocated to Western Nigeria in that court. I was appointed as the number two justice in the Western State Court of Appeal.

The High Court had what was disparagingly referred to as a 'judicial bonanza' because of the unprecedented number of appointments made to that court at the same time. It is not without significance that four of the six judges appointed at that time were retired during the collective retirement exercise of 1975.

The last straw in this series of calculated acts of humiliation came in July 1968 when the President of the Court went on leave for about three months. On the recommendation of the Advisory Judicial Committee in Lagos, the Supreme Military Council gave its approval for me to act for the President. The approval was suppressed by those unfavourably disposed towards me in Ibadan even though I was performing all the judicial and administrative duties which such acting appointment required. In the end, I was sworn in as the Acting President of the Court the day before Justice Kester, the substantive holder of the post, was due to resume duty. The only point on which the Military Governor refused to yield, under the heavy and consistent pressure of my adversaries, was that of the acting allowance to which I was entitled. He insisted that, since I had performed the duties, I should be paid the entire acting allowance from the date the President of the Court went on leave.

Meanwhile, to make sure that I would not be allowed to act for the President again, the appropriate section of the Constitution of Western Nigeria was amended. By that amendment, only the Chief Justice of the Region, and not one of the justices of the Court of Appeal, could, in future, act for the President of the Court of

Appeal. The futility of this exercise became apparent when, because of a fundamental disagreement over policy matters between the two, the President did not go on any long vacation leave again until both he and the Chief Justice retired from the State's judicial service. So the Chief Justice never, in fact, acted for Justice Kester as planned by my adversaries. Having regard to all these squalid manoeuvres, I am not surprised that no protest was raised when in 1976 this Court was abolished by the Federal Military Government and replaced by the present Federal Court of Appeal whose jurisdiction runs throughout the entire Federation.

At the time, I felt that someone somewhere was trying his best to annoy me into early retirement but I was equally determined to 'keep my cool'. I therefore absorbed every one of these calculated provocations with utter indifference. This, of course, annoyed my adversaries all the more.

Escape from this frustrating situation came in December 1968, when Sir Adetokunbo Ademola, then the Chief Justice of the Federation, asked the Government of the Western State for my services. I was to come and sit with him to hear some of the appeals pending in the Supreme Court at the time. After the first appeal, second and third requests were made for my assistance. The third request was for an indefinite period. I acted continuously as a justice of the Court from February to September 1969. On 2 October 1969, Sir Udo Udoma and I were both sworn in by the Head of State (General Yakubu Gowon) as substantive justices of the Supreme Court of Nigeria. My ordeal in Ibadan was over!

8 The Supreme Court

The Supreme Court is the country's highest court. While it has original jurisdiction in certain matters such as disputes between the Federal Government and State Governments or between two or more State Governments, its jurisdiction is mainly appellate. At the time of my appointment, it heard appeals from the High Courts of each of the States except the Western State where it heard appeals from the Western State Court of Appeal; now, with the abolition of the State's Court of Appeal, all appeals come to the Supreme Court via the Federal Court of Appeal.

Sir Lionel Brett had retired from the Supreme Court just before I was appointed a justice of that court in 1969. I had, however, worked with him when he was the Solicitor-General in the Federal Ministry of Justice. A confirmed bachelor with an addiction for snuff, he was a great lawyer, an erudite classicist, an outstanding judge, and one of the legal characters of post-war Nigeria. He was not given to suffering fools gladly but he had to suffer them all the same. His snuff-box was his most dreaded equipment in court. As soon as he took out the box in the middle of an appeal, opened it, put a small quantity of snuff in his nostrils, blew his nose into his unmistakeable red handkerchief, and told counsel to pause for a minute, counsel knew he was in trouble! The questions which followed from Sir Lionel usually determined the fate of the appeal. We all remember him for the exceptional clarity and elegance of his judgments, not to mention his inimitable gift of condensation. He was one of the very few justices of the court ever to write a dissenting judgment. When there was a further appeal to the Privy Council against the majority decision in one of the cases in which he dissented, we were not surprised that the Privy Council adopted the view which Sir Lionel had held and allowed the appeal.

Unlike the judges I worked with in the Western State Court of Appeal, the justices of the Supreme Court were daily practitioners of the art of gentlemanly restraint. There were always robust arguments among us and sharp disagreements that seemed to defy reconciliation. But underlying these differences was an atmosphere of cordiality that was rooted in mutual respect. It enabled some of us who were poles apart philosophically, to remain close friends.

Of all the justices with whom I worked in the Supreme Court, I enjoyed the best relationship, both intellectually and socially, with Justice G B A Coker. He was the supreme technician. Though he was a master of detail, he never allowed himself to become enmeshed in it. He could always discern, clearly and with precision, the broader issues involved in any appeal. He had, to an outstanding degree, the power of quick and correct decision based on the wisdom which comes from wide experience and a profound knowledge both of human nature and of the law. All his judgments were, as a consequence, tempered with a warm sense of humanity. He had a genius for friendship and for bringing out the best in all of us who had the privilege of working with him. His keen sense of humour made him a particularly delightful companion. It was a pity that he paid very little regard to the social conventions of the judiciary. His early retirement from the Bench was, indeed, a great loss not only to the judiciary of this country, but also to the development of the law.

Although the intellectual climate of the Supreme Court was rather severe and the workload, particularly at the time when I was appointed to the court, was very heavy, the work there was most stimulating. I was sometimes frightened by the measure of the responsibility which the Constitution has placed on the members of the Court, knowing as I did, that whatever was decided was final and conclusive until the decision was reversed either by the Court itself in a later case or by legislation.

One salient characteristic of our judicial establishment is its growing division into parallel systems of Federal and State courts with jurisdictions that sometimes overlap. The Federal Courts consist of the Supreme Court, the Federal Court of Appeal, and the Federal High Court. The State Courts are the High Courts, the Magistrates' Courts, the Native or Customary Courts, the Customary Court of Appeal, the Sharia Court of Appeal, the Area Courts, and the District Courts. The last three courts are established for and function in only the ten Northern States. There seems to be some overlap of jurisdiction in that courts such as the State High Courts are empowered by the Constitution to exercise jurisdiction in respect of matters within the exclusive legislative competence of the Federal Government in addition to their jurisdiction over purely State matters. We must not forget, however, that the final court of appeal for all these courts is the Supreme Court.

That Court exercises jurisdiction throughout the Federation. It consists of the Chief Justice of Nigeria and such number of Justices of the Supreme Court (not exceeding fifteen) as may be prescribed by an Act of the National Assembly. It is now provided in section 3 (1) of the Supreme Court Act (No. 12 of 1960) that 'the number of Justices of the Supreme Court shall be twelve'. The Court at present consists of the Chief Justice and ten Justices. The court is duly constituted if it consists of five Justices. In appeals against a decision in any civil or criminal proceedings on questions as to the interpretation or application of the Constitution, or in the exercise of its original jurisdiction, the court shall be constituted by seven Justices.

The Supreme Court has exclusive original jurisdiction in any dispute between the Federation and a State or between the States themselves if and in so far as that dispute involves any question (whether of law or fact) on which the existence or extent of a legal right depends. In addition to this, additional jurisdiction may at any time be conferred on the Court by any Act of the National Assembly provided that no such jurisdiction shall be conferred with respect to any criminal matter. The Court also has exclusive jurisdiction to hear and determine appeals from the Federal Court of Appeal.

In the exercise of its original jurisdiction, the Supreme Court administers law and equity concurrently and in the event of conflict, the rule of equity will prevail. The Court also observes and enforces the observance of any customary law which is applicable and which is not 'repugnant to natural justice, equity and good conscience, nor incompatible either directly or by implication with any law for the time being in force'.

In the exercise of its appellate jurisdiction, the Supreme Court may and does exercise any power that could have been exercised by the lower court concerned. It may and does sometimes order that the case be retried by a court of competent jurisdiction. In civil appeals, it has power to make any order necessary for determining the real question in controversy in the appeal. It has full jurisdiction over the whole proceedings as if the proceedings had been instituted in the Court as a court of first instance, and may rehear the case in whole or in part or may remit it to the court below for the purpose of such hearing. It may also give such other directions as to the manner in which the court below shall deal with the case.

The general setting of the Court is very sober,

drained of colour, and devoid of the excitement of a trial court. It contrasts in this regard with the pomp and pageantry that used to attend the quarterly openings of the assizes of the High Court in the old days. It is unfortunate that the parades, which had long been regarded as the outward manifestation of the administration of justice in the country, have now been scrapped. We used to get such parades when the Supreme Court went on sessions outside Lagos but the effect was never the same. This was probably because there were no red robes, no religious services, no fuss or drama, hardly any headlines; it is just plain black robes and grinding work!

The technique of the Supreme Court also is wholly different – as that of any court consisting of three or more judges must necessarily be – from the technique of a court of first instance where a judge sits alone. Mutual dependence supplants a hard-earned, carefully cultivated self-sufficiency. One of the greatest difficulties is for each member of the Court to keep in step with the other four. And you can imagine how difficult this can sometimes be when one is sitting as a member of a Full Court of seven justices, bearing in mind that it is provided in section 258(2) of the Constitution that –

'Each Justice of the Supreme Court shall express and deliver his opinion in writing, or may state in writing that he adopts the opinion of any other justice who delivers a written opinion'.

The effect of this provision is that each justice is an individual in his own right with the constitutional right to come to his own deliberate judgment while performing his judicial duties.

The curious thing, to borrow the words once used by Lord Justice Asquith –

'is how hitchlessly, . . . the system on the whole works. Dissent in particular is far less common than can be anticipated. In the great majority of cases, the three or five minds, after a period of oscillation and fluctuation, while material is being fed into them and argument is proceeding, settle down into a parallel course and advance smoothly to a common conclusion'.

From my experience in all the courts in which I have sat, it seems to me that the judicial process demands that a judge should exercise his jurisdiction within the framework of the relevant legal rules of practice and procedure and of the accepted modes of thought for ascertaining them. He must think objectively and dispassionately. He must learn to suppress his private feeling on every aspect of a case. On the whole, we judges must and do lay aside our private views in discharging our judicial functions. This is not always easy and it is only achieved through training, professional habits, self-discipline, and that sense of duty which makes a person become dedicated to the obligation with which he is entrusted. It is also true, however, that reason cannot control the subconscious influence of feelings of which such reason is unaware. Therefore, whenever there is ground for believing that such unconscious feeling may operate in the process of coming to a decision, or may lead other persons to believe that it is operating, a judge ought to decline to hear the case. He does this for a variety of reasons. The guiding and ultimate consideration is that the administration of justice is such a sacred trust that justice must not only be done but must be seen to be done.

The independence of the judiciary in Nigeria, which was badly dented under the military regime, has now been restored by the 1979 Constitution. The tenure of office of judges is now made more secure.

It is my view, however, that it is the respect which Nigerians have for the courts, in addition to the manner in which all judicial officers, including magistrates, comport themselves, that will sustain and safeguard the independence of the judiciary here in Nigeria.

Over one hundred years ago, an American (Alexander Hamilton) described the judiciary as the least dangerous branch of the government because it had no influence over either the sword or the purse, no direction of either the strength or of the wealth of the society, and could take no active resolution whatsoever. It also may truly be said that it had neither force nor will but merely judgment, and must ultimately depend upon the aid of the executive arm of the government even for the enforcement of its judgments. This feeling of helplessness vis à vis the courts in the United States, was re-echoed by Justice Samuel Miller in *United States v Lee* ((1882) 106 US 196 at page 223), when he said –

> 'Dependent as its courts are for the enforcement of their judgments upon officers appointed by the executive and removeable at his pleasure, with no patronage and no control of the purse or the sword, their power and influence rests solely upon the public sense of necessity for existence of a tribunal to which all may appeal . . . and the confidence reposed in the soundness of their decisions and the purity of their motives'.

I think the above observation is particularly relevant to all persons who are called upon to exercise judicial functions in a developing country where the executive, tasting power for the first time, thinks it can wield unlimited power indefinitely. The arrogance which results from such a mentality soon makes the executive intolerant of any person or body of persons which tries to put a constitutional limit to the scope of its power. Because of this, a judge who tries to put a limit on its excesses is sometimes referred to as a saboteur or a neo-colonialist or just too technical. This is why those who are appointed to high judicial office in any developing country must be persons who will retain the confidence of the public, in the long term, only through 'the soundness of their decisions and the purity of their motives'. They must be able and hard working in addition to being transparently honest.

But will the executive appoint such persons knowing that those appointed, with those criteria in mind, are likely to earn the confidence of society? This is where, in the Nigerian context, the calibre of the person appointed as the Chief Justice of the Federation and the Chief Judge of each State, as well as that of each of the members of the various Judicial Service Commissions is very important. The members of the Council of State, who must be consulted before appointments to the Federal Judicial Service Commission are made by the President, and those of a State Assembly, who are empowered to confirm appointments to the state Judicial Service Commission which are made by the Governor of the State, must be very vigilant. They should not shirk their duty to scrutinise the candidates for these Commissions properly and meticulously. Under no circumstances should the Commissions allow themselves to be unduly influenced by that innocuous phrase 'federal character of Nigeria', to the glaring exclusion of ability, experience and integrity, in the appointment of judges of the superior courts. To do so would not only make the litigant suffer injustice, it would also do incalculable harm to the administration of justice in Nigeria.

One of the highlights of my return to Lagos as a member of the Supreme Court in 1969, was the opportunity which the move afforded me to renew my close association with a friend of mine, Adekunle Ojora (now Chief Ojora, the Otunba of Lagos). After a successful career as a journalist and in broadcasting, Kunle Ojora's life took a significant turn in 1961, when he embarked on a business career first as a manager and later as group Public Relations Adviser to the United Africa Company of Nigeria Ltd, a post in which he was responsible for projecting the image of the company throughout Nigeria. In 1963, he was appointed a director of the company, a post which he held until 1967, when he resigned.

In 1967, he was appointed Chairman of the Nigeria National Shipping Line. That same year he also became the first General Manager and later the Managing Director of Wemabod Estates Ltd, a property development company owned by the then Government of Western Nigeria. He performed so brilliantly in both capacities that when he relinquished the two posts six years later, he was appointed the first Nigerian Chairman of Agip Nigeria Ltd, an oil company operating in Nigeria. He still holds this office in addition to many other chairmanships and directorships.

Chief Adekunle Ojora is rich, affable, intelligent, imaginative and articulate. A friendly man with important friends in high places, he is endowed with enormous energy and drive, and the ability to get things done, including things which, on the surface, appear impossible. He is, however, apt to be talkative and sometimes to give the impression of being able to achieve what he well knows he cannot possibly achieve no matter how hard he tries. For this reason, he has been regarded in certain circles as not completely reliable. Furthermore, his deference to those in authority or to those much older than he is could sometimes be mistaken by those who do not know him well for sycophancy. I, however, know that having first been a newspaperman and later a public relations adviser, he realised early in life that such people, or at least most of them, have their Achilles heel, in the form of a love of flattery! I cherish his friendship and his loyalty deeply.

I fondly recall the many stimulating and thought-provoking discussions which 'Kunle and I have had on the sandy beach at Tarkwa Bay near Lagos with our other friends, the brilliant and talented banker Sam Asabia and the late Abdul Atta, the equally brilliant conversationalist and fearless Secretary to the Federal Military Government. These discussions took place during the many happy and pleasurable weekends we all had at Tarkwa Bay during and after the Nigerian Civil War. In between these talks which were invariably about all the known or imagined ills of Nigeria, both economic and political, and about the best cure for them, I enjoyed my other hobbies of reading, walking, swimming, and cruising around in my speed-boat from Tin Can Island all the way to Badagry. These hobbies are dear to me and enable me to recharge my human battery for the next week's work on the Supreme Court Bench.

Early in 1977, Mr Gus Ehren, a senior partner of the accounting firm of Pennel Fitzpatrick & Company, decided to retire after spending twenty-five years in Nigeria. Many farewell parties were arranged in his honour. One of these parties was arranged by Dr and Mrs Abebe. Dr Chris Abebe was at that time the Chairman of the United Africa Co of Nigeria, a commercial octopus which controls the largest and most influential British trading and industrial group in Nigeria. Presumably because Gus Ehren had sat with me on the Ports Arbitration Board a few years earlier, my wife and I were among those invited to the Abebe's small dinner party at the Quo Vadis, a swanky restaurant at the top of Western House, an office-block overlooking Lagos harbour. The view of the harbour from the restaurant was enough to whet anybody's appetite that evening. Sitting at the head of our own end of the table was Dr Chris Abebe; on his right was Mrs Amy Ehren (the wife of the principal guest of honour). I was sitting on Dr Abebe's left. Justice Anyaegbunam, the Chief Judge of the Federal High Court, was sitting to the right of Mrs Ehren. Mr Pearse, another senior partner in the firm of Pennel Fitzpatrick, was on my left.

In the course of a lively conversation, I mentioned something about writing my memoirs. Justice

Anyaegbunam, who had appeared before me many times in his days at the Bar at Onitsha, when the Supreme Court used to sit there, intervened and said that I should include something about the Onitsha Bar because the members of that Bar had certain impressions about me. I replied that I did not know about those impressions. Justice Anyaegbunam promised to let me know about them later. When Mrs Ehren heard Justice Anyaegbunam say that he had appeared before me in the Supreme Court at Enugu many times, she turned to him and observed, with her characteristic innocence, 'Did he sentence you to prison?'. On hearing this question, Justice Anyaegbunam nearly dropped his spoon into his soup! I was most intrigued by the observation but too flabbergasted for words. Dr Abebe fortunately broke the silence by bursting into true Nigerian laughter. We all followed suit and laughed heartily at this profound but rather off-the-mark observation. A good time was thereafter had by all.

Before we left the restaurant, Justice Anyaegbunam promised to let me have a written version of those impressions. The following are the rather flattering impressions which he has given of my contribution to the development of the law in Nigeria.

'The name of Justice Fatayi-Williams has been known by many members of the Onitsha Branch of the Nigerian Bar Association even before they met him. This is so because Justice Chuba Ikpeazu and L O V Anionwu, a former Nigerian Ambassador to Italy, were at Cambridge University together with Justice Fatayi-Williams and they always spoke highly of him. The impression created of him was that he is a very thorough and meticulous man who insists on the best in whatever he sets out to do. In the early fifties when he was a Crown Counsel in Enugu, the senior members of the Onitsha Bar that met him in and out of Court also thought highly of him. As a law officer,

104

they said he was very firm and at the same time fair in prosecution.

When he was elevated to the High Court Bench in the then Western Nigeria, this sterling quality was very manifest. In his court, cases were tried on the dates they were fixed unless there were extenuating circumstances. At that material time, his judicial division covered Ogwashi-Uku, Agbor and Asaba. This afforded many members of the Bar from Onitsha an excellent opportunity to know and appreciate Justice Fatayi-Williams more. They learnt a great deal from him. Among the things they admired most was his punctuality. He always sat in his court promptly at 9 am. One of the lawyers once remarked that one could regulate one's wrist watch by the time Justice Fatayi-Williams stepped into court. All lawyers from Onitsha, at the time I was in practice, were of one mind that Atanda, as he is sometimes fondly called, reads his case files from cover to cover with the result that when you are leading your witness-in-chief, you happen to introduce any fact not pleaded, he would promptly stop you and ask you to show the paragraphs of your pleading in support of the evidence which you proposed to lead. Nothing in your statement of claim or statement of defence would escape his eagle eyes. He is very precise and as such encourages economy of language in submissions before him. He frowns at verbose argument. In spite of all these, he is very humane and polite in court. To young lawyers, he is always kind and tolerant.

After he was appointed a justice of the Supreme Court it was always a pleasure to appear before the panel of Supreme Court Justices in which he is a member. Just as he did with the case files in the High Court, he masters his records of appeal no matter how voluminous. No minute point of fact or law will escape his attention. With this in mind, lawyers in Onitsha take great pains in studying their record of appeal, checking all the facts as contained in the record and all the relevant law whenever they are going to argue any appeal before the Supreme Court. I recall that one of the legal practitioners, after spending a sleepless night preparing his appeal, was very tired the following morning; when asked by his colleagues why he was so tired, he replied that he was getting ready for Justice Fatayi-Williams as he was going to appear before the Supreme Court in a few days and he would not like to be rattled by being asked by the Justice to reconcile the evidence of a witness on page 15 of the record with that of another witness on page 70 of the record and the remarks of the learned trial judge on pages 210 and 230. I personally had experienced the kind of searching question similar to the one anticipated by the lawyer as stated above. Sometimes it could be a stormy passage but it was always very refreshing and rewarding in the end.

Outside the court, Justice Fatayi-Williams is quite a different person. In the circle of his colleagues and close friends he is a jolly good fellow; his stern serious look disappears completely; that aura of austerity which perhaps made George Orwell in his essay 'England your England' describe a High Court judge in these words

> "The hanging judge – that evil old man in scarlet robe and horse hair wig, whom nothing short of dynamite will ever teach what century he is living in . . ."

completely evaporates. His friends and associates know very well that beneath that horse hair wig and scarlet robe there is a heart of gold that is at the same time very warm and most friendly.

During one of the Supreme Court sessions in Enugu, the Onitsha Branch of the Nigerian Bar Association, gave a luncheon party for the Supreme

Court justices then on session. I was privileged to sit next to Justice Fatayi-Williams. Some few tables away from us was Mr Tony Iguh (as he then was; he is now a High Court judge in Anambra State) with some other lawyers. He was having some discussion with them. As he was talking, he was gesticulating and pointing his finger to his small audience as is usual with him. I did not know that Justice Fatayi-Williams was watching him. Then the Justice turned to me and asked, "What is the name of that lawyer talking and pointing his finger as he spoke?" I replied and said, "He is Mr Tony Iguh, one of our best advocates." He then smiled and said that if he had not always noticed him do this in court while making a serious point he would have thought that he was having a serious row with those sitting at his table. Everyone at our table roared with laughter. Since then, this has been a common joke in the Onitsha Bar.

The members of the Onitsha Branch of the Nigerian Bar Association read the judgments of Justice Fatayi-Williams with relish. They regard them as pieces of legal literature.

His reserved judgment in *Emejokwue v Okadigbo* is epoch-making. It is one of the leading judgments of the Supreme Court. There are many such judgments. Now, let me refer to two of what I consider his most important dissenting judgments. They are *Jammal Steel Structures Limited v African Continental Bank Limited* (1973) SC 77 at page 101 and *Mobil Oil (Nigeria) Limited v Federal Board of Inland Revenue* (1977) 3 SC53 at page 97. Apart from the wealth of legal knowledge very succinctly expressed in the two dissenting judgments, the style, the beauty, and the rendering of the judgments are to my mind superb. In the *Jammal* case, he expounded with the skill of a master the rule of *ejusdem generis* and that of *copulatio verborum indicat acceptatione in codum sensu.*

The short facts in the *Mobil Oil* case were that Mobil Oil Nigeria Limited (the appellants) delivered to the respondents, the Federal Board of Inland Revenue, their audited returns. The appellants were assessed on the figures shown on the returns and they accordingly paid. Later on, the respondents wrote stating that the rates of profits declared for the years of assessment then in question had been less than expected from the size of business carried on by the appellants in Nigeria. The respondents then taxed the appellants on "the assessable profits for both years of 15% of the turnover for each year". The appellants objected. After exchange of some correspondence between the parties, the rate was reduced from 15% to 10%. The appellants, not satisfied with this assessment, appealed to the Federal Appeal Commissioners. They dismissed the appeal and confirmed the assessment. The company then appealed to the Federal Revenue Court. The Federal Revenue Court reduced the percentage from 10% to 8%. The company was still not satisfied. They, therefore, appealed to the Supreme Court. The appeal was finally dismissed and the decision of the Federal Revenue Court was confirmed. Justice Fatayi-Williams dissented and gave his reasons. At the tail end of his judgment, he came out with one of his bold and characteristic statements. It runs thus –

". . . it will be a sad day, I think, when a company, whether Nigerian or expatriate controlled, can be assessed to pay tax on a percentage of its turnover simply because its management is poor, or because its management is good and efficient by reason of the fact that it pays higher salaries and looks after its employees better than those of other companies manufacturing or marketing the same products. As the Emperor Tiberius aptly put it in 'Sentonius Lives, Ch.XXXI' many years ago –

'*Boni pastoris case tenders pecus, non
deglubere.* (The good shepherd shears
his flock, not flays it).'

This dictum to my mind is sound and full of
common sense'.

The above observations are distinctly flattering. It is,
nevertheless, gratifying to know what eminent lawyers
like Justice Anyaegbunam think of my humble contribution to the development of the law in Nigeria. Justice
Anyaegbunam is not the only member of the profession
who has been very kind in his assessment of my work.

In March 1973, the Supreme Court went on sessions to
Enugu. At the first sitting of the court, the Attorney-
General and Commissioner for Justice, East-Central
State, gave us a short welcome address in which he
devoted a paragraph to me. This paragraph, which I
must confess pleases me, reads –

'It is needless to say that we always appreciate Your
Lordship's sound exposition of the law. In these
sessions we anxiously look forward to judgments
similar to those of Justice Fatayi-Williams which have
enriched our Law Reports and many of which have
remained a classical analysis of the competing claims
for supremacy between our customary laws and the
received English law. Nor have we forgotten that His
Lordship made great contributions to the revision of
the current Laws of the Western State. We are very
pleased that he is on this panel'.

Among the appeals over which I presided in the
Supreme Court, I recall most clearly that of the late Chief
Pere Cole (the Pere of Kumbowei Clan of the Sagbama
Community in Western Ijaw Division) and six others as
appellants and the Shell/BP Petroleum Development
Company of Nigeria Ltd, as respondents, because of the
curious turn of events when the appeal was being heard.

In January 1972, Chief Pere Cole and six others had claimed agains Shell/BP of Nigeria as follows –

'The plaintiffs claim against the defendants the sum of £60,000 (sixty thousand pounds) being a fair, reasonable and adequate compensation payable by the defendants to the plaintiffs for the damage done to plaintiffs' property that is to say the Sagbama Creek – a Creek over which the plaintiffs had exercised and continued to exercise customary rights from time immemorial whereby the defendants during their dredging operation of the said Creek caused damage to plaintiffs' gravel, sand, juju shrines, erosion to plaintiffs' land and occasional permanent loss of fishing rights on or about May 1971 within the jurisdiction of this Honourable Court'.

After evidence had been taken, judgment was delivered in May 1975. The trial judge gave judgment for the plaintiffs and awarded them, by way of compensation, a total sum of N45,840 with N750 costs. The defendants appealed against this decision and at the same time asked the court for stay of execution of the judgment pending the hearing of the appeal before us in the Supreme Court. For some inexplicable reason, the trial judge refused the application for stay and ordered Shell/BP to pay the judgment debt and costs to the plaintiffs. Shell/BP, as everyone in Nigeria knows, is good for much more than N45,000. Be that as it may, Shell/BP, by virtue of provisions of our Rules of Court, applied further to the Supreme Court for a stay of execution. Meanwhile, the plaintiffs had levied execution, significantly at a weekend, on the properties of Shell/BP in Port Harcourt. As a result, Shell/BP frantically paid to the plaintiffs the total amount of the judgment debt with costs. When we in the Supreme Court heard the application for stay of execution a few days later on 13 October 1975, we ordered that Chief Pere Cole and his co-plaintiffs should pay into the

110

Supreme Court, within fourteen days, the total sum of N46,593.55k paid to them by the defendants upon and as a result of the execution of the writ of attachment in the court below. Thereafter, the matter was adjourned for the records of the proceedings in the lower court to be prepared in the court below and sent to us for the hearing of the appeal. The actual hearing of the appeal commenced on 17 October 1977. During the course of the argument, we discovered that the Order of the Court of 13 October 1975 had not been complied with by Chief Pere Cole and his people. We thereupon gave them three days to pay in the amount to the Register of the Supreme Court pending the final determination of the appeal. This was not done. Thereupon, we ordered that a bench warrant should be issued on Chief Pere Cole and the other six plaintiffs to show cause why they should not be committed to prison for disobeying the order of the Supreme Court. The bench warrant was duly executed and the seven of them, who were all in Warri Division, were brought to Lagos and detained in Kirikiri Prison.

At the further hearing of the case on 7 November 1977, counsel for the respondents produced four cheques comprising the entire amount from different banks and indicated that two of the cheques were certified bank cheques while the others were not, where-upon, as the presiding judge, I told him that the money would be paid into the account of the Supreme Court immediately, and as soon as it was cleared, the respondents would be released from custody because our primary intention was to see that no order of the Supreme Court was flouted. We had no desire to keep anybody in custody for a minute longer than necessary. Counsel thereupon told us that there were not enough funds to cover one of the cheques and asked for further adjournment. I replied that he should go and see that enough funds were raised to pay the entire amount into the bank and that as soon as we were informed, whether on the next day or the next week or the next fortnight that all the cheques had been cleared, we would empanel a special sitting of the Court for the purpose of releasing the respondents from prison immediately. Meanwhile, I noticed that some well-dressed and well-groomed gentlemen were sitting in court. Learned counsel for the respondents told me that all of them were the illustrious off-spring of the offending respondents and that he wanted some time for consultation with them. They asked for ten minutes and we agreed to their request. When they returned to court, these 'illustrious sons', through learned counsel, applied to the court that the case should be adjourned to 19 December 1977, by which time they hoped that the entire amount would have been raised and paid into court. It was also indicated to us that they, who were entitled to their share of the compensation, were never informed by their elders that the compensation had been collected. The elders merely collected the money and shared it amongst themselves! At this stage, we got the impression that these illustrious sons wished the court to teach their elders a lesson by keeping them in custody for some time at least. I commended them for their sense of responsibility and told them that they were a credit to their country. I also told them that we all operate under the rule of law and that no man, no matter how highly placed, was above the law of this country. I ended my observation by pointing out to them that once the rule of law is jettisoned in any democratic country, anarchy would be the only beneficiary.

Chief Pere Cole and his six associates went back to gaol while their dependants went to look for the balance of the money. By the time the matter came up before us on 19 December 1977, Chief Pere Cole had died. The other six defendants were eventually released from custody after the court had been informed that all the amount involved had been paid back into court. Thus ended the saga of the late Chief Pere Cole and his six associates. It should be stated, however, that when the substantive appeal was heard later, the defendants/appellants were only partially successful with the result that the remaining plaintiffs (all associates of Chief Pere Cole) were able to recover more than half of the money which they were ordered to pay into court pending the determination of the appeal!

In June 1966, the National Military Government (later known as the Federal Military Government) promulgated the Public Officers (Investigation of Assets) Decree. The main purpose of the Decree was to enable the Head of the National Military Government to require public officers to declare their assets whenever he thought that such declaration was in the public interest. It also provided for the verification and ascertainment of the assets so declared. After considering such report as may be submitted to him by those responsible for the verification, the Head of the National Military Government might, in appropriate cases, appoint a tribunal to inquire into and report on the assets of the public officer.

Where the report of the tribunal disclosed that an officer had corruptly or improperly enriched himself or some other person, the Head of the National Military Government could order the forfeiture of the assets to the State. The powers conferred above on the Head of the National Military Government were also exercisable by the Military Governor of a State subject to certain prescribed conditions.

Pursuant to the provisions of Edict No 5 of 1967, which was later replaced by the Decree referred to above, the Military Governor of the Western State set up a tribunal of inquiry into the assets of certain categories of public officers in the State. The late Justice Olajide Somolu (then Chief Justice of the State) was appointed the chairman of the tribunal. Among the assets enquired into by the tribunal were those of Mr E

O Lakanmi and his daughter, Mrs Kikelomo Ola. After taking evidence from all the parties concerned, the tribunal ordered as follows –

'(1) Under the provisions of section 13 subsection (1) of Edict No 5 of 1967, it is hereby ordered that Mr E O Lakanmi, Kikelomo Ola (his daughter) and all others who may be holding properties on behalf of or in trust for any of them, shall not dispose of or otherwise deal with any of the said properties of whatever nature (ie lands, houses, etc) whether standing in their names, or in any other of their various names and/or aliases, until the Military Governor of the Western State of Nigeria shall otherwise direct.

'(2) In particular, it is hereby ordered that the said E O Lakanmi or his said daughter mentioned above shall not operate their individual bank accounts by means of withdrawal therefrom without the consent of and only to the extent what the Military Governor of the Western State shall permit in writing.

'(3) It is hereby further ordered that all rents due on the properties of the said persons from henceforth shall be paid by the tenants thereof into the Western State Subtreasury at Ikeja or the Treasury at Ibadan, until the Federal Military Government shall direct to the contrary, pending the determination of the issues involved in the investigation into the assets of all those concerned.

'(4) Attention of all persons concerned, and/or their partners, co-directors, shareholders or nominees, or anyone who may like to have business transactions with them for any reasons and in any manner whatsoever is invited to these orders and penalties provided in section 13 sub-section (2) of the same Edict in case of the infringement thereof'.

Being dissatisfied with this Order, Mr Lakanmi and his daughter applied to the High Court for an order of *certiorari* to have that part of the Order that restricted them from using, disposing of or dealing with their properties, and directed that all rents accruing from their properties be paid into the Western State Treasury in Ibadan or the Sub-treasury in Ikeja, be quashed. The High Court dismissed the application after finding that there had been no breach of natural justice, that the tribunal had acted properly, and that, in any event, the action could not be brought by *certiorari*.

Still dissatisfied they appealed to the Western State Court of Appeal which struck out the appeal for want of jurisdiction. Still not satisfied, they appealed to the Supreme Court (Ademola, CJN, Coker, Lewis, Madarikan and Udo Udoma, JJSC) which allowed the appeal and set aside the various orders after holding –

'(a) that Edict No 5 of 1967 and Decree No 45 of 1968 dealing with the forfeiture of assets were *ultra vires* and null and void;

(b) that Decree No 51 of 1966 covered the whole field for the investigation of the assets of public officers and that being the case Edict No 5 of 1967 was *ultra vires;*

(c) that the doctrine of necessity applies when the Decree sought to amend the Constitution of the Federation;

(d) that since the civilian government handed over power to the interim military government, there could not be any question of a revolution;

(e) that there was a clear separation of powers in the Constitution as between the judiciary and the executive; and

115

(f) that the provisions of Decree No 45 of 1968 disclose a usurpation of the judicial powers of the courts of the Federation.

On hearing of this decision, delivered on 24 April 1970, the Federal Military Government reacted strongly by promulgating the Federal Military Government (Supremacy and Enforcement of Powers) Decree of 1970 (Decree No 28 of 1970), which came into force on 9 May 1970. The provisions of this unfortunate Decree, which marked a clear erosion of the powers of the judiciary vis à vis the executive, are as follows –

'WHEREAS the military revolution which took place on January 14 1966 and which was followed by another on July 29 1966, effectively abrogated the whole pre-existing legal order in Nigeria except what has been preserved under the Constitution (Suspension and Modification) Decree 1966 (1966 No 1):

AND WHEREAS each military revolution involved an abrupt political change which was not within the contemplation of the Constitution of the Federation 1963 (hereafter referred to as "the Constitution of 1963"):

AND WHEREAS by the Constitution (Suspension and Modification) Decree (1966 No 1) there was established a new government known as the "Federal Military Government" with absolute powers to make laws for the peace, order and good government of Nigeria or any part thereof with respect to any matter whatsoever and, in exercise of the said powers, the said Federal Military Government permitted certain provisions of the said Constitution of 1963 to remain in operation as supplementary to the said Decree:

AND WHEREAS by section 6 of the said Constitution (Suspension and Modification) Decree 1966, no question as to the validity of any Decree or any Edict (in so far as by section 3 (4) thereof the provisions of the Edict are not inconsistent with the provisions of a Decree) shall be entertained by any court of law in Nigeria:

116

AND WHEREAS by Schedule 2 of the said Constitution (Suspension and Modification) Decree 1966 the provisions of a Decree shall prevail over those of the unsuspended provisions of the said Constitution of 1963:

NOW THEREFORE THE FEDERAL MILITARY GOVERNMENT hereby decree as follows –

1. (1) The preamble hereto is hereby affirmed and declared as forming part of this Decree.

    (2) It is hereby declared also that –

    (a) for the efficacy and stability of the government of the Federation; and

    (b) with a view to assuming the effective maintenance of the territorial integrity of Nigeria and the peace, order and good government of the Federation, any decisions, whether made before or after the commencement of this Decree, by any court of law in the exercise or purported exercise of any powers under the Constitution or any enactment or law of the Federation or of any State which has purported to declare or shall hereafter purport to declare the invalidity of any Decree or any Edict (in so far as the provisions of the Edict are not inconsistent with the provisions of a Decree) or the incompetence of any of the governments in the Federation to make the same is or shall be null and void and of no effect whatsoever as from the date of the making thereof.

    (3) In this Decree –

    (a) "decision" includes judgment, decree or order of any court of law, and

    (b) the reference to any Decree or Edict includes a reference to any instrument made by or under such Decree or Edict'.

It cannot be too strongly stressed that the Federal Military Government was too sensitive about the decision. As a result, they over-reacted unnecessarily. It will be recalled that the Western State Court of Appeal of which I was a member at the material time held that it had no jurisdiction to interfere and thereby supported the order for the forfeiture of the assets of both Lakanmi and his daughter Kikelomo Ola. We therefore struck out the appeal against the order for forfeiture which had also been earlier confirmed by the Western State High Court. However, by their judgment delivered on 24 April 1970, the Supreme Court reversed our decision. Looking back, I still disagree with their decision in the matter. I thought that our decision in the Western State Court of Appeal was the right one to take having regard to the validating effect of the Forfeiture of Assets, etc. (Validation) Decree (Decree No 45 of 1968). Be that as it may, for the Federal Military Government to deprive the Supreme Court, as it had done by Decree No 28 of 1970, of practically all its ultimate judicial power to interpret the provisions of the Constitution vis à vis a Decree, is to say the least, a violent assault on the rule of law which it had categorically professed, at various times both to Nigerians and to the outside world, to support and maintain.

If the Federal Military Government had only intended to make the Supreme Court judgment ineffective, and not to humiliate the court, it could have saved future orders for the forfeiture of the assets of corrupt public officers by a suitable amendment to the section of the Constitution which provides for the payment of compensation for property of any person compulsorily acquired by the State. This amendment, made with retrospective effect, could be by way of another proviso to the section stating that no compensation would be payable in respect of properties compulsorily acquired pursuant to the finding of a tribunal set up to inquire into the assets of public officers.

In the alternative, but I agree that this is the extreme, the Federal Military Government, if it had so wished, could have suspended the entire Constitution and ruled by martial law. We would have known then that no Constitution was in force and that nobody could have looked to any of its suspended provisions for the protection of his or her fundamental rights. In fact, there would have been no such rights to protect.

Not having taken either of these measures, it was indefensible to react to a decision of the Supreme Court which, as the Constitution stood at the time, the court was empowered to give. A constitutional lawyer like myself found it difficult to accept a situation where the military regime, in one breath, allowed the provisions dealing with both the powers of the Supreme Court and with fundamental rights to remain in force, and in another breath, promulgated a Decree which provided that any decision by any court of law which purported to declare that a Decree or an Edict is invalid shall be null and void.

In retrospect, it is ironical that it is because the military regime had given itself these extreme powers that it was relatively easy for it to retire some judges of our superior courts when the Gowon regime was ousted in July 1975. This unfortunate Decree, it will be recalled, was enacted at a time when Dr TO Elias, who was later appointed the Chief Justice of Nigeria, was the Attorney-General of the Federation. In this exalted and powerful position, where to my knowledge he was venerated and highly respected by the regime, he could have used his influence in favour of caution and moderation. There was no indication that he did. About two months before the judges had been retired, he himself retired from the office of Chief Justice on grounds of 'ill-health'. Not long after this rather sudden retirement, he was appointed a judge of the International Court at the Hague.

Some time in June 1972, Dr Elias, the Chief Justice, with the concurrence of the other justices, mandated me to go to London and order suitable ceremonial robes, befitting the dignity of the Supreme Court, for the Chief Justice and justices of that Court. Armed with this mandate, I went to Ede and Ravenscroft Ltd, the robe-makers of Chancery Lane, London, where, after discussions, we were able to produce between us the design which is now that of the ceremonial robe of the Chief Justice and justices of that Court. The robe of the Chief Justice is made of black silk damask with train, fully trimmed with gold ornaments on the sleeves and plate lace. That of the justices of the Supreme Court is also made of black silk damask but without train and with less fully trimmed gold ornaments on the sleeves. It is also trimmed with gold oakleaf lace. I must admit that I am proud of this new design which my colleagues accepted without any dissent. It is, I think, by far better, less flamboyant and much more attractive than the heavily laced one which is worn in other countries.

The wearing of wigs and gowns by the members of the Bench and the Bar in Nigeria has been criticised in some influential circles in Nigeria as neo-colonialist. After spending over twenty years on the Bench of the superior courts here in Nigeria where wigs and gowns are worn, I think that the wearing of these professional wigs and gowns lends dignity and solemnity to the proceedings of these courts. In any case, why pick on the judges and the lawyers? These critics might as well tell the bishops and the members of the armed forces and the police to discard their robes or braided uniforms and wear 'agbada' instead. Even our Obas might as well be asked to do away with their crowns!

The simple fact is this. Throughout the ages, certain aspects of one culture have been influenced by contact with aspects of other cultures. Thus the language, art-forms, music, farming methods, mode of dress and uniforms of one cultural group have influenced those of another cultural group. This had led to what is now known as the cross-fertilisation of cultures. In time, this cross-fertilisation, with continuous modification to suit

120

local conditions, has resulted in the creation of a related but original culture. This is what has happened here in Nigeria with respect to the wearing of wigs and gowns, and indeed of uniforms generally, by members of the legal and other professions. Let us therefore leave well alone for the moment. There is nothing neo-colonialist about retaining it. We have here with us the pressing problems of poverty, health, and education to cope with at the moment without bothering about what judges and lawyers wear in court.

The last thirty-six years will not be forgotten in the legal history of Nigeria. They are the age of the first Nigerian High Court Judge (Sir Olumuyiwa Jibowu), the federalisation of the judiciary, abolition of appeals to the Privy Council, appointment of Nigerians as Queen's Counsel (later replaced by Senior Advocates of Nigeria), limited law reform, legal aid, and of John Idowu Conrad Taylor!

I first met J I C (as he was popularly known throughout Nigeria) in 1942 at a houseparty at the Akinsemoyins in Breadfruit Street in Lagos. He had just returned from the United Kingdom where, in addition to qualifying as a lawyer, he had also been awarded a blue in boxing at Oxford. He read law at Brasenose College, Oxford. At the time I met him, I was preparing to go abroad to read law myself. J I C struck me as young, bright and confident. My heart warmed to him but he hardly noticed me. When I met him again on my return from the United Kingdom six years later in 1948, he had established himself, in his own right, as one of the brightest young lawyers in the country. At that time, his father, the late E J Alex-Taylor, was known as the 'cock of the bar' because of his 'no-nonsense' style of advocacy. Without doubt, J I C was an illustrious son of an illustrious father.

J I C and I became good friends almost immediately. I was a guest first at his father's country house at Ojokoro and later at his own attractive mansion at Ikeja on many occasions. The association meant a lot to Irene and myself and we valued it highly. J I C, at that time, had three passions – the law, cricket, and fast cars. Within thirteen years he had reached the top of the legal profession so we were not surprised when he was offered appointment as a judge of the High Court in the Western Region in 1955. At cricket, he captained the Nigerian side against other West African countries on at least four occasions; the cap fitted him very well because he was a first-class sportsman. With his collection of fast sports-cars, including an Aston Martin, he was the darling of the Lagos taxi-drivers!

J I C gave up cricket and his collection of cars when he became a High Court judge, although he always had one fast car at least. His career on the Bench was brilliant. He was meticulous and hardworking, his output was prodigious. He took immense pains to get to grips with all the cases which came before him. Both lawyers and litigants swore by the quality of his judgments. In the late fifties, his only son was struck down by polio. He was so affected by this that he visited the boy, who was then no more than a toddler, every day in the University College Hospital at Ibadan. Eventually, he became a recluse and hardly went anywhere.

In 1960, he was appointed a justice of the Federal Supreme Court. Consequently, he left the Western Region and returned to Lagos. His tenure in the Court was noted for his strong views, his partiality for doing substantial justice in the face of legal technicalities, and his abhorrence of sharp technical points. Indeed, he wrote a number of dissenting judgments because of his laudable attitude to the administration of justice.

In 1964, J I C left the Supreme Court to become the Chief Justice of the High Court of Lagos. He became a legend in that court by his hard work, his unapproachability, and most important, by his unswerving dedication to the cause of justice and fair play. When it came to administering justice, he was no respecter of persons or public authorities. His sudden death, in November 1973 was, indeed, a great loss both to the nation and to the legal profession. His great contribution to the development of the law is, however, acknowledged through the 'Taylor Lectures' delivered in a series every year by eminent jurists, either from Nigeria or from abroad, under the auspices of the University of Lagos where he once held the post of Chairman of its Provisional Council.

Early in 1970 the Federal Military Government decided to take over the ports of Warri, Calabar and Burutu which were at that time being operated as privately owned concerns by expatriate firms. Before the takeover the port of Warri was being operated mainly by Holts Transport Ltd. Calabar was run by Palm Line Agencies Ltd (a division of the United Africa Co of Nigeria Ltd or UAC), African Properties Ltd, and Elder Dempster Agencies (Nigeria) Ltd. The port of Burutu, which was the largest in area of the three ports, was under the control of the UAC.

In order to implement this decision the Government passed the Ports (Amendment) Decree (Decree No 55 of 1969). By this Decree a Fifth Schedule was added to the Scheules in the Ports Act (Cap 155 of the Laws of the Federation) which had the effect of transferring the rights, obligations, interests and liabilities of the companies controlling the ports to the Nigerian Ports Authority. The Decree also established an Arbitration Board whose function was to determine the total value of the assets to be transferred in each of the ports and to apportion compensation among the companies. The Chairman of the Arbitration Board was to be a justice of the Supreme Court, nominated by the Chief Justice. The Chairman was to sit with two other arbitrators, one appointed by the Federal Commissioner for Transport in consultation with the Federal Commissioner for Justice and the other by the companies operating the ports. In March 1970 I was named as Chairman of the

123

Board. Mr D O Dafinone (now a senior Senator in the Nigerian Senate) was appointed by the Commissioner and Mr Alfred Ehren by the port operators. They are both chartered accountants; Mr Ehren is an Englishman.

The first public sitting of the Arbitration Board took place on 24 March 1970. In my opening statement I stressed that, notwithstanding the formula by which the members of the Board were appointed, our primary duty was to act independently and impartially, always bearing in mind that independence is the essence of the arbitral function. I also emphasised the fact that as arbitrators we were not merely valuers but also had judicial functions to perform and like any other tribunal performing such functions we had a duty to act justly and fairly. The Board had the power to lay down its own rules of procedure to which I urged the parties to conform in the interests of expediting our deliberations.

The Board sat in Lagos, Warri, Calabar and Burutu. We took evidence in all these places and inspected the relevant assets in each of the ports. Having submitted our valuations to the Government, the port operators were paid the amounts awarded to them.

If only for its historical interest, I think our finding with respect to the assets claimed by the UAC in the port of Calabar is worth recapitulating here. The UAC claimed an interest in properties at Calabar known as Millerio Wharf, Jackson Wharf, Cliffe House, Holmes Beach, and Matilda Beach.

The basis of the claim to an interest in Millerio Wharf was described in the report prepared for the Board by the Company as follows:

'The title to the land is derived from a grant dated 6 March 1886 made between King Duke Ephraim IX and Alexander Henderson as Agent for Alexander Miller Brother and Company and their successors conditional upon them continuing to trade from the

124

property. Should the Grantees declare that they no longer wish to trade the ground shall revert to the Grantor. A rental of £25 per annum is payable to the Duke Town families'.

On the basis of this grant, the company according to the report regarded their title as one of leasehold in perpetuity being a land grant held under Native Law and Custom. It was pointed out at a later hearing that the company could not hold land under Native Law and Custom, and this description was therefore deleted and the following substituted for it:

'The title is based on right of possession from 1886 for as long as the annual rent of £25 is paid.'

The Board rejected the Company's contention that its interest amounted to 'a perpetually renewable tenancy or lease'. It was our view that

'Whenever one person holds land of another, and there is no express limitation or agreement as to the term for which it is to be held then, if the rent is a yearly rent the tenancy is deemed to be a tenancy from year to year. The general rule applicable in cases of compulsory acquisition of land, and which would appear to be applicable here, is that if a tenant has no greater interest than as a tenant from year to year the interest of the tenants is not purchased. . . . If the UAC remained in possession to the end of 1969 (the takeover was on 1 December 1969), the year for which rent was last paid, they will get nothing for they no longer hold any interest to which any value can be attached to the land. In the circumstances, we cannot place any value on this nebulous interest which the UAC claimed to have in the land at Millerio Wharf'.

The UAC's claim in respect of Jackson Wharf was based on a Certificate of Possession dated 1 August 1889 and declared before the Consul for the Rights of Benin and Biafra. The rent payable under the Certificate was £25 per annum and this title, like that for Millerio Wharf, was amended during the hearings to one based 'on right of possession from 1889 for as long as the annual rent of £25 is paid'. Here again the Board found the UAC to be no more than yearly tenants with no interest on which any value could be placed. A similar finding was made in respect of Cliffe House and Holmes Beach the titles to which were based on a Certificate declared before the Consul in 1889. There was, however, some dispute between the UAC and the Ports Authority as to the value of the Cliffe House buildings, the plant and machinery they contained, and the dry dock on Holmes Beach. The UAC valued the assets at a total of £N28,542 while the Ports Authority argued for a valuation of £N16,800. The buildings had been damaged during the Civil War and much of the plant was unserviceable. The Board valued the assets at £N18,800.

The title to the property at Matilda Beach was based on a document reading as follows:

'This is to certify that the Establishment on Old Calabar River known as 'Matilda Beach' and the property of Messrs Thomas Harrison and Company is in all respects held by them in undisturbed possession, and in full accord with the Customs and Usages of the river and that the Annual Rent payable to the King and Chiefs is –

> One Hogshead of Rum and
> 30 Thirty Bags Salt
> Dated Old Calabar 2nd day of
> August, 1889
> Sgd H H Hartje

Declared before me and signed in my presence by H Hartje at the British Consulate Old Calabar this twelfth day of August One thousand eight hundred and eighty nine.

Sgd. E.H. Hewatt
Her Brittanic Majesty's
Consul for the Bights
of Benin and Biafra'.

according to the UAC report this payment in kind was
changed to a payment of £25 per annum at a later and
uncertain date. The UAC regarded the title 'as one of
user for as long as the rent of £25.00 per annum is
paid'. There was no evidence from the UAC as to how
they came to occupy the land. Another document referred to the beach as being 'the property of Messrs
Thompson Harrison and Company' and there was
nothing to show that this company had transferred its
interest in the land to the UAC or that the UAC was its
successor-in-title although there was evidence that the
UAC had been in occupation of the Beach for a considerable length of time with the consent of the families
to whom the annual rent of £25 was paid. The Board
found, as it had in relation to the other Calabar properties, that the UAC could only be yearly tenants with no
interest in the land to which any value could be
attached. The Company would therefore only be
entitled to compensation for development it had under-
taken on the land. This development consisted of a
number of dilapidated warehouses which the Board
valued at a nominal £N200.

The valuation of the Burutu Port complex was a
more involved and difficult matter. By agreements
dated 11 April 1895 and 10 August 1898 the Royal
Niger Company purported to buy land along the Forca-
dos river near Burutu from the Head Chief and Chiefs
of that town. In 1916 the Niger Lands Transfer Ordinance (Cap 149 of the Laws of Nigeria 1948) vested all
the lands and rights belonging to the Royal Niger Company within the Southern Provinces of the Protectorate
in the Governor in trust for the British Crown. By section 4 (1) of the Ordinance, however, some specified

lands remained the property of the Royal Niger Company (or the Niger Company Ltd as it was by then called) and these exceptions to the general provisions of the Ordinance included part of the Burutu properties.

In 1935 the Niger Company Ltd sold all the lands it held under the Ordinance, among which were the Burutu properties, to the Nigerian Properties Company Ltd. In 1957 this company went into liquidation and its assets passed to the UAC which held them in June 1970 when they vested in the Ports Authority by virtue of the Ports (Amendment) Decree. These assets comprised freehold and leasehold interests in the land, the Port (consisting of the wharves, warehouses, dockyard, offices, management housing, junior staff housing, a supermarket and a hospital), plant and machinery, households and office furniture, hospital equipment and stores. The principal purpose of the Port of Burutu had been to handle the cargoes transported by river to and from Northern Nigeria and the Northern Cameroons. Recently the import and storage of materials used in the rapidly expanding oil exploration industry had become increasingly important. The wharves and warehouses were well equipped, as was the dockyard which was complemented by a range of workshops housing plating, welding and fitting departments as well as facilities for shipwrights, coppersmiths, blacksmiths and riggers. There was also a modern machineshop, a substantial office block and a fuel oil bulk storage installation. Road access to all parts of the dockyard was good and there were comprehensive electricity, water and compressed air networks. In addition to ship repair, building and conversion work the dockyard was equipped to handle a wide range of general engineering orders.

The UAC valued these assets at a total of £N1,502,059. The Ports Authority did not file any detailed reply to this valuation but stated that it would base its case on a valuation of £N350,000 which was the sum for which the UAC had agreed, subject to contract, to sell what was described as 'the Burutu complex' to a potential purchaser in 1969. This contract was never completed and there had, therefore, been no sale. The Board was unable to accept the valuation put on the assets by the UAC, in which an alarming degree of arbitrariness was apparent. The experts who had valued the various assets for the UAC had used different methods and arrived at widely disparate figures. When asked whether his attitude to a valuation would depend on whether he was valuing the property for a buyer or for a seller one of their witnesses replied revealingly:

'My Lord, in theory, it does not. We are professionals and we do our very best to give impartial advice. In practice, perhaps it is slightly difficult because this is not a science, it is not a piece of mathematics, it is a question of opinion. The advice that I have given the UAC in this matter is as impartial as my psychology allows it to be'.

Counsel for the Ports Authority asked the Board to value the assets at £N350,000 on the ground that this was the sum that had been offered for them on the open market but as this offer had been accepted subject to contract the Board felt that it could not reasonably be regarded as representing the Port's 'open market value'. A third possible valuation of the assets emerged in the form of an offer of £N500,000 which had been made for the Port by the mid-Western State Government earlier in 1970. The Board also considered a fourth figure – £N596,768 – which was the value attributed to the assets in the UAC's most recent certified accounts.

We were of the opinion that there could not in fact be any 'market' for the Burutu Port complex in the sense in which one speaks of a 'market' for shares or cement or beer. The two offers for the Port had, in any case, been made in somewhat ambiguous and artificial circumstances. The Board therefore rejected the whole concept

of a 'market value' in favour of the more realistic valuation
provided by the accounts, which reflected the particular
circumstances in which the UAC found itself at the time of
the Decree. The Board therefore valued the Burutu Port at
£N597,000.

On the last day of the proceedings of the Arbitration
Board I thanked all those who had participated for their
co-operation. In reply, Mr Godfrey Amachree, who had
appeared as counsel for the Ports Authority observed:

'My Lord and Gentlemen of the Board, on behalf of the
Ports Authority management, counsel and others, I
would like to reciprocate your thanks and to thank you
all for the extremely fair manner in which you have
conducted these arbitrations. Your courtesies, patience
and understanding of the case presented both by the
relevant companies and the Ports Authority have in no
small measure encouraged those of us who have had a
very difficult assignment. Evidence of your sense of
justice and fairplay has been evinced by the announcement you have made in the award just made to the UAC
in Burutu. I fought strenuously to make you do something else, but I must say that I agree entirely with the
award myself.

We will remember this arbitration in that many of us
have learnt a lot. It is my first experience with valuers
and also it gave me an insight into the workings of the
minds of chartered accountants. I am grateful for the
opportunity and also extremely grateful to you all for
what you have done for us'.

In January 1972, I received a letter from the Principal
Secretary, State House, informing me of my appointment
by the Head of State as a member of a committee which
had been set up to examine the case of Mr Peter Anyansi
with the following terms of reference –

'to re-examine the case of the suspension of Mr Peter
Anyansi's Warrant as Assistant Chief Commissioner

and the decision of the National Scout Council to expel him from the Association, and to submit your findings and recommendations for His Excellency's consideration'.

Originally, this committee, which consisted of Sir Adetokunbo Ademola (then Deputy Chief Scout), the Rt Revd S I Kale, Mr Justice H U Kaine, and myself, was to have sat under the chairmanship of Sir Adetokunbo Ademola. However, before we could commence the assignment, I received another letter from the Principal Secretary informing me that as the Deputy Chief Scout was unable to serve on the Committee, the Head of State had appointed me the Chairman of the said Committee. The inquiry was intended to be an administrative one. Fortunately for us, all the decisions taken either by the Chief Commissioner or by each of the committees or Council concerned, were based on the documentary evidence made available to them. In the case of the Chief Commissioner, the decisions were reduced into writing either in letters forwarded to the Head of State or in a report tabled before and discussed by the various bodies connected with scouting which the Chief Commissioner had deemed it desirable to inform. In particular, a quantity of documentary material was referred to the Management Committee of the Boy Scouts Association, the Committee of the National Scout Council and the National Scout Council itself. The contents of these documents were considered before the decisions, later recorded in the minutes of the meetings of each of these bodies, were taken. Copies of most of the minutes and of the documents on which the discussions and decisions were based, were made available to us. Mr Anyansi was not asked to appear and did not appear before any of the committees which recommended his dismissal from the Association or the National Scout Council which decided to dismiss him. Since the role of the committee was limited by its terms of reference to that of 're-examination', and bearing in mind that the inquiry should be purely administrative, the committee decided, after due deliberation, to limit its enquiry to the documentary material available to all the scouting bodies or individuals concerned. We had no doubt in our minds, after going through all the minutes and documents submitted to us, that this was, by far the best course in an inquiry of this nature. Our decision was therefore based solely on the interpretation which could usefully be placed on them. No oral evidence was therefore called for in our consideration of the matter. Eventually, we submitted our report to the Head of State. Our conclusions and recommendations are as follows –

'1. In view of the deterioration in the relationship between Mr Anyansi and the Chief Commissioner, not to mention his obvious lack of tact in his dealings with the Management Committee, we recommend that his resignation from the office of Executive Commissioner should be allowed to stand, save that this resignation, for the purpose of regularity, should be accepted with retrospective effect, not by the Chief Commissioner or the National Secretary of the Association, but by the Management Committee which recommended his appointment. The decision should then be communicated to Mr Anyansi by the National Secretary who, we understand, is also *ex officio* the secretary of the Management Committee.

2. The power to appoint an Assistant Chief Commissioner is vested in the Chief Scout by virtue of the provisions of Article V clause 2 of the Constitution of the Association. There is no provision in the Constitution for the suspension or withdrawal of the Warrant of such appointment. As we have pointed out earlier, rules 72 and 73 of the Boy Scout Rules which provide for suspension apply only to Scouters. It is, therefore, doubtful whether the Chief Scout

could suspend or withdraw the Warrant of an Assistant Chief Commissioner once he is appointed. We venture to say, with respect, that, as the Constitution stands, once a person is appointed to that office, he is entitled to hold the office for the statutory period of five years unless he relinquishes the office of his own volition or he dies. It may be desirable, perhaps, to amend the Constitution to enable the Chief Scout to remove, for just cause, all the officers of the Association which he is empowered to appoint.

3. For the above reasons, the suspension of Mr Anyansi's Warrant by the Chief Commissioner is tainted with illegality and is, for that reason, of no effect whatsoever. We accordingly recommend that a directive should be given that all documents relative to that decision should be expunged from the records of the Association. Finally, we recommend that no action should be taken on the recommendation, made by the Chief Commissioner to the Chief Scout in his letter of 7 April 1971, that the Warrant of Mr Anyansi's appointment as Assistant Chief Commissioner should be withdrawn.

4. The decision of the National Scout Council taken at the meeting held on 2 July 1971, for the reasons which he had given earlier in this report, is both unconstitutional and patently irregular. Even assuming, without conceding, that the Council had the power to take this decision, it seems to us that when weighed against his forty-five years contribution to scouting in Nigeria, the shortcomings of Mr Anyansi which we have spotlighted in this report, though reprehensible, do not justify his dismissal from the Association. We recommend that the Council should be so informed. We also recommend that the Council should be directed to expunge from its record of that meeting all the proceedings and decisions relative to his dismissal.

5. Finally, in the interest of scouting in Nigeria, all efforts to bind and heal the Association's wounds, inflicted by this sharp rift between Mr Anyansi on the one hand and the Chief Commissioner and the members of the Management Committee on the other, may not be out of place. The Deputy Chief Scout may be of assistance in this respect. We therefore strongly recommend that he should be requested to take on this assignment with all deliberate speed'.

Although we submitted our recommendation to the Head of State (Gowon) as far back as October 1972, no action was taken on it until after the death of Mr Anyansi sometime in 1974. It is, however, gratifying to note that the Boy Scout's Movement in Nigeria has been reorganised along the lines recommended by us with the late Ben Okagbue as the new Chief Commissioner of Scouts. He succeeded Justice S O Lambo who has since retired.

In 1972, Sir Adetokunbo Ademola retired after serving as the Chief Justice of Nigeria for fourteen years. Like all persons who have held high judicial office for a long period, he had his own share of powerful enemies. But even his greatest enemy could not deny his dedication and the air of maturity and experience which he gave to the administration of justice in the highest court in the land. It was unfortunate that soon after his retirement he accepted the Chairmanship of the National Census Board, a thankless assignment which brought him right into the centre of the bitter controversy over the 1974 census figures which were eventually rejected *in toto* by the Federal Military Government. Be that as it may, Sir Adetokunbo served Nigeria well. I am glad to know that he is enjoying his retirement notwithstanding his recent appointment as the Chairman of the Commonwealth Foundation based in London.

Sir Adetokunbo was succeeded as Chief Justice of

Nigeria by Dr T O Elias in February 1972. Before coming to the Supreme Court, Dr Elias had been the Attorney-General of the Federation continuously, except for about six months, since 1958.

In addition to being a brilliant academic lawyer of international repute and an author of many books on various aspects of the law in Nigeria, Dr Elias is also a first-class administrator. It was therefore not surprising that he came to the Supreme Court with clear ideas about improving the administrative structure of the court. Within a few months of his taking office the entire structure was dismantled and reorganised. A research section was set up. The annual publication of the *All Nigeria Law Reports* was re-activated and brought up to date. Publication of the monthly judgments of the Supreme Court was introduced. These monthly publications became extremely popular both at home and abroad. He appointed me as chairman of the Law Reporting Committee which he set up soon after he assumed office.

Having been the Attorney-General of the Federation for so long, Dr Elias, however, found it rather difficult to accept and absorb dissent from his colleagues on the Supreme Court Bench. As I could hold very strong views when I felt that it was necessary to do so, I sometimes found myself holding views diametrically opposed to his own. It took him some time to accept this as a way of life in the court, particularly as the Press were in the unfortunate habit of referring to the sittings of the Court as being 'presided over by the Hon Dr T O Elias *assisted* by Justice Fatayi-Williams and Justice Sowemimo'. It never occurred to the Nigerian Press that each of the justices of the Supreme Court, including the Chief Justice, is an individual in his own right with respect to the performance of his judicial duties. As no justice is subordinate to the Chief Justice or to another justice in this respect, each one of us is free to dissent from the individual or collective views of the others. It

135

is to the credit of Dr Elias, however, that he never held a permanent grudge against any of us who had to disagree with him on occasions. He was a very loyal Chief Justice and we all gave him our loyalty in return.

It was unfortunate that he had to retire suddenly in August 1975, before his reorganisation of the judiciary of the country had been completed. One aspect of the reorganisation which he conceived, and in respect of which I was allowed to play a major role later, was in the establishment of the Federal Court of Appeal. In order to determine finally what form this intermediate court between the Supreme Court and the State High Courts should take, Dr Elias succeeded in getting the Government of the United States of America, with the consent of our own Head of State, to arrange for me to go to the United States and observe at first hand the actual workings of the United States Supreme Court and also how the work of the Circuit Courts of Appeal has affected the heavy work-load of that court. I reported what I had seen and heard on my return. Based on my report, Dr Graham-Douglas (then the Attorney-General of the Federation) in collaboration with Dr Elias, produced the first draft Decree establishing the Federal Court of Appeal. Unfortunately, they both left office before the draft was finalised. Before leaving office, however, Dr Elias had assigned to me the duty of producing a new set of Supreme Court Rules which would reflect the new procedure to be followed in respect of appeals to the Supreme Court from the Federal Court of Appeal after that court had been established. The new Supreme Court Rules came into force on 1 September 1977.

There is no better proof of the dismal error of the Federal Military Government in the retirement of Dr Elias from the office of the Chief Justice of Nigeria in 1975 and his replacement with a non-Nigerian than the announcement in 1982 of his appointment as the President of the International Court of Justice at the Hague following the death of Sir Humphrey Waldock of Britain who had been the President of the Court. It is significant that this elevation of Dr Elias was made within seven years of his appointment as a judge of that Court. Indeed, a prophet is not without honour save in his own country and among his own people!

Dr Elias was succeeded as Chief Justice of Nigeria by Sir Darnley Alexander, then Chief Judge of the South-Eastern State (now the Cross-River State), one of the twelve States which then made up the Federation of Nigeria. When the appointment was announced by the then Military Administration in August 1975, many well-meaning Nigerians found it strange that a country which could boast of about two hundred indigenous judges in all its superior courts of record, and which for the last two decades or so has been exporting Chief Justices and judges to other African countries as part of its technical assistance to these countries, cannot find an indigene to head the judiciary of Nigeria.

The result of this ill-advised appointment is that all the innovations made by Dr Elias during his short tenure of office – the research unit, the publication of the monthly judgments of the Supreme Court, the supreme effort made by him to bring the publication of the *All Nigeria Law Reports* up to date, were either abandoned or suspended or allowed to lapse. Instead, those of us in the Supreme Court were treated to a repeated demonstration of excessive *deference* towards those in authority.

I very rarely see Dr Elias these days. This is because he spends more time at the Hague than in Nigeria. On the few occasions when we have come together again, I have got the impression that he listened to what I was saying rather absentmindedly. I felt, probably without justification, that the cares of the International Court were pressing heavily upon him. The years which had sat lightly on him in the past now seemed to weigh him down. Of course, this is often the case with men who

137

have set their lives towards the distant glow of one high and glowing ambition. When the hilltop of their ambition is reached and there is nowhere further to climb, and all that is left is to pile more on the flame and keep the fire burning, they just sit beside their radio or in front of their television set and grow old. Where their ambitious blood warmed them up before, it is the tropical heat which now does it from without! I cannot, however, imagine Dr Elias sitting beside a radio or in front of a television set for any length of time. He is more likely to spend most of his time in his well-stocked library rummaging through his books or writing new works.

One afternoon during the latter half of 1974, I received a 'phone call from Chief Justice Elias. He asked me to see him in his official residence in Ikoyi Crescent, Lagos. When I arrived, my colleague Justice Sowemimo was already there. Dr Elias gave us in a few words the reason for this urgent meeting. Apparently, earlier that day, Dr Elias had received a 'phone call from General Gowon who was then the Head of State complaining about the manner in which the courts in the country were being used for the indiscriminate swearing of affidavits in which allegations of corruption were made against public functionaries.

Prior to this 'phone call, one of Gowon's Commissioners, the late Joseph Tarka, had been forced out of office because of the facts deposed to in one of these 'offending' affidavits sworn to by one Daboh. At the time the complaint was made by the Head of State, another affidavit had been sworn by one Aper Aku in which Joseph Gomwalk, then the Military Governor of Benue-Plateau State, had been accused of corruption on a vast scale.

When Dr Elias asked for our views about the legality and propriety of the swearing of such affidavits when no cases or proceedings were pending in court, I pointed out that we should be reluctant to get involved because, over the years and by long usage, Nigerians have been swearing on oath to affidavits as to facts within their knowledge. I cited the example of sworn affidavits or declarations as to age, loss of driving licence, and recently in support of declaration of assets by public officers. Justice Sowemimo supported me in my counsel of caution. The Chief Justice appeared to be in agreement with us.

Certain influences must have been unleashed between our meeting and the next morning because, at nine o'clock that day, Dr Elias called another meeting of all the justices of the Supreme Court. Present at this second meeting were the Chief Justice, Justice Dan Ibekwe, Justice Ayo Irikefe and myself. Justices G B A Coker and Sowemimo, for some reason, were absent. Justice Udo Udoma, I think, was then out of the country. When the matter of the affidavits was reopened, I found that all the other justices were in favour of banning the swearing of affidavits sworn to when no cases were pending in court. Again, I suggested that we should not be involved but all my entreaties fell on deaf ears. As an alternative, I suggested that somebody should be encouraged to start a test case by way of a claim for a declaration explaining that this would enable all the courts to look at the legal implications closely. Again, nobody would support me. In the end, I informed the Chief Justice and my colleagues, pointblank, that, on first reaction, I did not share their views on placing a ban on the swearing of affidavits. The meeting ended on that note.

Still not satisfied with the so-called majority views of my colleagues in the Supreme Court, the Chief Justice, who was also the Chairman of the Advisory Judicial Committee – a body set up by the Constitution for the appointment of and the exercise of disciplinary control over the judges of all the superior courts in the country – called for a meeting of the Committee to discuss the same issue. We were told through a press-release issued by the Chief Registrar of the Supreme Court that this Committee, whose members include the Chief Justice of Nigeria as Chairman, the Attorney-General of the Federation, the Chief Justices (as they were then called) of each of the twelve States, the President of the Federal Revenue Court, and the Grand Khadi, had unanimously decided that, except in connection with proceedings already pending in court, the courts would no longer allow affidavits to be sworn in court by aggrieved citizens.

At this stage, the Nigerian Bar Association waded into the controversy and contended that the members of the Advisory Judicial Committee were wrong in their decision and that no law in Nigeria prohibited the swearing of such affidavits. Even Dr Onogoruwa, the able, versatile, resourceful and well-informed legal adviser to the *Daily Times of Nigeria* joined in on the side of the lawyers in a thought-provoking feature article on the issue in the *Daily Times*. The matter soon became a public issue. Some people thought that the image of the judiciary was tarnished by the resultant controversy.

In retrospect, it was unfortunate that Dr Elias allowed himself to be involved in the controversy. He should have accepted my advice and allowed the matter to go to court where, after arguments had been adduced, a well-considered pronouncement on the law on the point could have been made, both at first instance and later on appeal if necessary. His outstanding reputation would have remained intact thereby.

Later purges of public officers after the overthrow of the Gowon regime in July 1975, purges which included State governors, heads of federal and state ministries and non-ministerial departments, army officers, customs officials and university lecturers, illustrate how widespread corruption was in the country at the time when Gowon 'phoned Dr Elias and complained bitterly to him about the indiscriminate swearing of affidavits. It will be recalled that ten out of the twelve military governors of the ousted Gowon regime were found guilty either of corruption or gross impropriety in the performance of their duties, or blatant abuse of office. Only Brigadier Mobolaji Johnson of Lagos State and Brigadier Rotimi of the Western State left office without any known blemish. The pressure behind the Gowon complaint can therefore be imagined.

Looking back, it seems that, in objecting to the swearing of affidavits as requested by Gowon, Dr Elias and some of my colleagues, including the State Chief Justices and the other members of the Advisory Judicial Committee which supported them, unnecessarily but innocently got themselves involved in a situation the scope and dimensions of which they could not possibly have comprehended at the time they were stampeded into what eventually turned out to be a monumental attempt at a cover-up.

The last military administration took over from that of General Gowon after a bloodless military coup on 29 July 1975. I was in London at the time of the coup where I stopped over on my way to Kuala Lumpur, capital of Malaysia, to attend a Conference of the Commonwealth Magistrates which was being held there during the first half of August 1975. I thought I would be recalled after the coup but as I was not I proceeded to Kuala Lumpur as planned. Dr Elias, the Chief Justice, who was to have led the large Nigerian delegation was in Trinidad at the time. He returned to Nigeria immediately only to retire, on grounds of ill-health, from the office of Chief Justice a few weeks later. I eventually headed the Nigeria Delegation to Kuala Lumpur.

After the Conference I returned to London to start my annual holiday. After spending two weeks in London, I went to Spain to join my wife who had just arrived there from Nigeria. Two days before I left for home, I read in the London *Times* that Sir Darnley Alexander, the West Indian Chief Justice of the South-Eastern State (now renamed Cross River State) had been appointed Chief Justice of Nigeria. He succeeded Dr Elias.

I arrived back in Nigeria on 28 August 1975. On 30 August, I received a telephone call from Dodan Barracks. The aide who put the call through informed me that Brigadier Obasanjo, who was then Chief of Staff, Supreme Headquarters, would like to see me right away. Knowing that a number of public officers, including some judges, had been retired during the last fortnight, I thought the message heralded my own departure from the Supreme Court. I, therefore, emptied all the contents of the drawers of my writing desk, including the personal files in my steel cabinet, into a travelling case which I kept permanently in my chambers for carrying books necessary for my research at home. The packing took only a few minutes. Thereafter, I proceeded to Dodan Barracks full of apprehension!

At Dodan Barracks, I was ushered with minimum delay into the office of the Chief of Staff. Chief Rotimi Williams was in the office. The Chief of Staff was also there. He was very kind and civil to me. He told me officially of the appointment of Sir Darnley as the new Chief Justice. He then explained that because he had heard that I was going to resign my appointment as a justice of the Supreme Court, he wished to assure me, with the authority of the late Brigadier Muhammed, the then Head of State, that the appointment was no reflection on my ability or integrity on the Supreme Court Bench. He said they had to do what they did because of other drastic measures which they proposed to take and in respect of which they would not wish to involve me.

He confirmed that Alexander's appointment was for only three years. I replied that I could not have told anybody that I was going to resign because I had just returned to the country. I also said that quite apart from the fact that Alexander was a personal friend of mine, he did not appoint himself Chief Justice, so why should I walk out at that time when there were only two justices (Sowemimo and myself) left in the Court. Incidentally, Sir Udo Udoma was ill in hospital in England at the time, Justice Irikefe was at the head of the States Creation Commission, while the late Dan Ibekwe had been appointed the Attorney-General of the Federation. To be honest, I did contemplate leaving the Court but after the Chief of Staff had spoken to me with such commendable candour, I decided to stay on, if only to assist the new military administration to keep the machinery of justice working. I did add, however, that the Nigerians who had spoken to me could not understand why, out of the two hundred or so Nigerian judges serving in the various courts in the country, no one could be found suitable for appointment as Chief Justice particularly since, over the years, we have supplied other African countries with Chief Justices and judges. The Chief of Staff repeated that they had to do what they did and that there were cogent reasons for their action. Chief Rotimi Williams was present throughout these exchanges. I got the impression, because he said very little, that he was asked to be present only as a witness.

On my return to the Supreme Court, Phil Maha, my personal secretary, could not look me in the face as I passed through his room. He honestly thought I had been retired, so serious˘ and indiscriminate was the retirement exercise at the time. I asked him to come in after I had returned to my desk. When I told him that I was still at work as usual, he was so pleased that he grinned spontaneously from ear to ear. He was very loyal to me throughout the time he worked for me. I was pleased when he was later appointed an Information Officer in the Federal Ministry of Information.

The Alexander period as Chief Justice of the Federation expired at the end of August 1978. We gathered that it has been extended but for how long nobody seemed to know. During the three years when he was Chief Justice, a lot of changes took place in the country's judiciary. Some of these changes are for the better, others are too early to assess, while others are, clearly and definitely, misguided. Although I have always thought him to be an able and conscientious lawyer, a first-class legal draftsman and a hardworking and experienced, if slow, administrator, he seems to me, at the best of times, talkative, pettifogging and constantly conscious of the fact that he is not a Nigerian but a guest in a country which has given him immense scope to realise his ambition. His eternal gratitude sometimes beclouds his judgment and prevents him from standing firm and resisting pressure. The 'three years contract appointment' did not help the situation.

Within a month of the appointment of Sir Darnley Alexander as Chief Justice, many judges of the superior courts in the country were retired for no known reasons. While some of those affected by this exercise deserved to be retired, others could not be explained. Each judge was more or less left to fit the reason for his own retirement into any of the published heads – corruption, ill-health, diminishing productivity, old age, and, I think, abuse of office. My colleague, Justice G B A Coker, one of the most able and senior justices in the country, heard of his own retirement for the first time over the Lagos radio network. It is significant that within a year of his retirement, he was appointed the sole Commissioner for the revision of the Laws of the Federation by the same government which had retired him compulsorily from office. One cannot help feeling that had the last military administration realised at the time of the exercise that most litigants who lost a court case or accused persons who have been convicted have a grudge against the presiding judge and that they tend to peddle unfounded allegations against him as a result,

144

they would have been less enthusiastic about his removal without cast-iron proof of the allegations made against him.

Without doubt, these peremptory retirements undermined, to an irredeemable degree, the confidence which the people of this country have had, since colonial days, in the judiciary. Those of us who have worked, first as lawyers and later as judges in the five earlier administrations of Macpherson, Robertson, Azikiwe, Ironsi and Gowon, all of which preceded the Murtala Muhammed administration, felt that an edifice which took years to erect had been hastily demolished without thinking, before the demolition, whether the material for its reconstruction was readily available. It did not occur to those responsible for the exercise that the stability of any country which is not governed by a dictator depends on the respect which the government and people of that country have for their judicial institutions. This is why revolutions hardly occur in countries where the courts and the judges are put on a pedestal by the executive who proclaim their independence of thought and action regularly to the people they govern. The reason for such stability is not far to seek. So long as the masses of any country know, or are made to believe, that the judiciary of their country is strong, respected, and independent enough to curb the real or imagined excesses of their government, they will put up with a lot of decisions which they do not like or approve of because they know that if they are pushed too far, there is a third organ of government, the judiciary, to which they can go for redress. Therefore, for the sake of stability, it is in the interest of whatever government is in power, to sustain the image of a fearless and independent judiciary.

In the Nigerian context, it would have been far better for the new military administration of Murtala Muhammed to have asked the judges concerned to resign of their own volition if it was thought that, for

145

some valid reasons, they ought not to remain in office. By so doing, the judges would have left office with some dignity and decorum. It would not have been necessary to destroy or tarnish, as they did, the image of the institution of the judiciary on which the doctrine of the rule of law is based. The British, without doubt, left us something of value; we devalued it with a stroke of the pen!

It is doubtful whether the Chief Justice of Nigeria was ever consulted about these retirements. Of course, he himself was in time removed from the High Table at State banquets and from the front row at State functions. Although we were regularly told that the judiciary was still the third arm of the government and that the Chief Justice was at the head of it, he was left, sometimes, to fend for himself, either on a side-table at a State banquet or in the second or third row at other State functions. It was always sad and sometimes disconcerting to notice his lonely posture on television, sitting in splendid isolation, during some of these grand occasions. To my knowledge, this is the first time in the history of this country where the Chief Justice has been so shabbily treated. All previous administrations, be it civilian or military, treated the head of the judiciary with respect. It is doubtful whether a Nigerian Chief Justice would have put up with this constant and regular humiliation which must have delighted many a senior civil servant knowing, as I do, what members of that cadre feel about the judges of the superior courts of this country.

Be that as it may, the reaction and sense of shock of the people of Nigeria to this humiliation of the judiciary by the last military administration can be best assessed from the way the members of the Constitution Drafting Committee and those of the Constituent Assembly have bent over backwards to restore and protect for future generations the independence of the judiciary and the dignity of the judges.

In between my hobbies of reading, walking and swimming and cruising around the creeks in our speedboat, I enjoy my Tuesday visits to the Metropolitan Club for lunch.

According to its Rules, 'The objects of the Club shall be –

(a) the association in a social club of gentlemen, resident in Lagos, who are at present, and are likely to continue to be, major contributors to the progress of Nigeria;
(b) the maintenance of Club premises in Lagos and the provision of facilities for the use of members of the Club and their guests'.

The Rules also limit the number of ordinary members of the Club to 350.

At present, the Chief Executive of practically every major industrial and commercial concern based in Lagos, Apapa, or Ikeja is a member of the Club. So also are the heads of all the major petroleum companies and the largest insurance companies. The deputy chief executives of the largest ones are also members. The professions of Law, Medicine, Accountancy, Banking, Engineering, Insurance, Architecture, Journalism, Estate Valuation and Management, Quantity Surveying, and Pharmacy are also represented by the cream of these professions in Nigeria. We also have a number of foreign envoys the nationals of whose countries have sizeable investments in Nigeria. At least four Justices of the Supreme Court are members. So also is a former judge of the International Court at the Hague. Dr Elias, a former Chief Justice of Nigeria and now the President of the International Court is an honorary member.

In addition to the Tuesday luncheons at the Club and the sometimes noisy but always educative discussions which go with them, facilities are provided in the Club for private luncheons on any other day of the week and for private cocktail or dinner parties any evening during

147

the week. Because of the very high calibre of the membership, there is hardly any topic on which another member or his guest needs enlightenment that there is usually at least one other member who can help. This is because most members have travelled widely all over the world and have been exposed to a wide range of experience. The Club bar on a Tuesday afternoon is lively, with a continuous cross-fertilisation of ideas by idealists, realists, hard-headed business executives and pipe-smoking intellectuals. Those who have nothing to contribute to the topic under discussion just stand by, listening and learning. I have learnt a lot from these exposures.

Indeed, I considered it a very great honour when I was asked, in 1977, if I would accept an invitation from the Club at its next Annual General Meeting that year, to succeed Sir Adetokunbo Ademola as the President of the Club. Sir Adetokunbo, who had been President of the Club since it was founded in 1959, had apparently decided, of his own volition, to relinquish the post that year. I accepted the invitation and was accordingly unanimously elected President of this most prestigious Club in July of 1977.

Without doubt, the Club is serving the purpose for which it was founded. It is hoped that this trend will continue because we certainly need such a Club in Lagos.

9 Top of the tree

In about the third week in July 1979, my colleagues and I of the Supreme Court heard on the Federal Radio Corporation network news, for the first time, that the term of service of Sir Darnley Alexander as Chief Justice would expire on 24 August 1979, and that he had been re-assigned from the office of the Chief Justice to the Chairmanship of the Law Reform Commission. The news was rather surprising since none of us had any inkling of it.

Be that as it may, it provided a good opportunity for the local rumour-mongers to get into top gear. All sorts of rumours were being peddled all over the place. For my part, I came to the conclusion that if anybody whom I considered not suitable was appointed Chief Justice, I would simply give in my notice and retire from the Bench. True enough, a particular name kept cropping up all over the place. Consequently, I drafted a letter giving notice of my intention to retire from the Supreme Court Bench with effect from 1 September 1979.

On 21 August, however, I received a telephone call from the Cabinet Office in Lagos followed by a letter, at about 9.00 am, from the Secretary to the Federal Military Government. The contents of the letter read –

'My Lord,
    His Excellency the Head of the Federal Military Government, Commander-in-Chief of the Armed

Forces, has expressed the wish to meet you in his office *today* at 2.30 pm. I should be grateful if you would please try and attend.

Please confirm that you will attend.

Yours sincerely,
(signed)
J E UDUEHI
Permanent Secretary,
Cabinet Secretariat,
for Secretary to the Federal
Military Government'.

I confirmed in writing that I would attend the meeting at 2.30 pm on that day as requested.

On arrival at Dodan Barracks I was ushered into the Office of the Head of State, General Olusegun Obasanjo. We exchanged greetings and sat down. A discussion then followed. From the discussion, I gathered that he was of the opinion, though not strongly held, that within the last year or so I had not been co-operating fully with the Chief Justice. I explained my own side of the story to him and he seemed to be satisfied. After talking generally about the affairs of the country, he got up all of a sudden and congratulated me on being appointed as the Chief Justice of Nigeria. It was like a bolt from the blue! It was totally unexpected, and, for the first time in my life, I was at a loss for words. He watched my discomfiture with relish and delight. After about three minutes, I recovered my composure and thanked him and the Supreme Military Council for conferring this high honour on me. I promised to do my best and to rededicate my life to the service of my country. Thinking it was time I left, I asked the Head of State whether it would be alright if I told my wife and my mother of the preferment. He looked at his watch – the time then was about twenty-five to four – and replied, 'The news of the appointment will be on the air at 4.00 pm, and I doubt whether you would be able to reach them by then'. Anyway, I thanked him once again and left Dodan Barracks.

Inside the car, just outside the iron gates of Dodan Barracks, I told my official driver, Patrick Egbeola, and my police orderly, of the appointment because I just could not keep it all to myself. I had to talk to somebody. Without thinking, my driver let go of the steering wheel and started clapping with joy! On getting to the house, I rushed upstairs to tell my wife who was then ill in bed with typhoid. Because of the state of her health, she was not really impressed and I felt grossly deflated. She just said, 'Oh! good', and went back to sleep again. I thereafter went to the family house at Alhaji Issa Williams Street, Lagos, to tell my mother. The information did not make a great impression on her either. She just congratulated me and left it at that.

The appointment was surprising, to say the least, and because of this it was well received, I think, throughout the country. As soon as the appointment was announced over the Federal Corporation network, the vibrations were seismic. The newspaper response to the appointment boosted my ego considerably. Eventually, I was sworn in as the Chief Justice of Nigeria at Dodan Barracks at a very quiet but dignified and impressive ceremony by the Head of State.

From the 22 August 1979, the date after my appointment was announced, hundreds of congratulatory messages poured in from all parts of Nigeria and also from all my friends overseas. Among the six hundred or so letters and telegrams which I received, I would like to refer to just two: one was from a former Head of State, the Hon Dr Nnamdi Azikiwe, the Owelle of Onitsha, and it reads as follows –

'My dear Chief Justice,
    I write to contribute my humble quota to the congratulatory messages which must have inundated you since the announcement of your well-deserved elevation.

It was heart-warming news and I am very happy that a jurist of your stature now heads the highest court of our beloved nation.

I must make one confession and you are at liberty to believe it or not. But it is the truth.

Three weeks before the announcement of your elevation, I was involved in a serious dialogue with a compatriot, who was kind enough to place at my disposal a copy of your short address to the graduands who were called to the Nigerian Bar by the Body of Benchers on 16 July, 1979.

What attracted my attention was your charge to those who might aspire to hold high judicial office. You said *inter alia:*

'Finally, a few of you may be called upon in the future to hold high judicial office. In all your endeavours in this respect try to uphold, at all times, the rights of the individual whether against other individuals or against the State.

Strive always to sustain the rule of law and also to maintain and protect our Constitution bearing in mind that once the rule of law is jettisoned, anarchy will be the only beneficiary. On every occasion when you are called upon to adjudicate between the poor and the rich, the individual and the State, remember that time-hallowed guideline of the judiciary: *'Fiat justicia et ruant coeli'* – 'Let justice be done though the heavens fall'.

As parting advice, I commend to you, in your journeys through life, via this consuming and demanding profession, this prayer –

'God, grant me the serenity
To accept the things I cannot change,
Courage to change the things I can
And wisdom to know the difference'."

' I frankly told my friend that it would be a calamity for Nigeria if in selecting a new Chief Justice your claims were side-tracked. Thank God, my intuition did not end as a phase of wishful thinking.

In conclusion, please accept my sincere congratulations with my warmest regards and my honest belief that your appointment has reinforced my unalloyed faith in the independence of the judiciary and the sanctity of the rule of law.

As a former Head of State, I should be credited with having a modicum of intelligence to know what I am talking about.

Believe me to be,
Very sincerely yours,
    (signed)
NNAMDI AZIKIWE
    The Owelle'

The second letter was from Chief Obafemi Awolowo. Although it is short, I, nevertheless, detect personal knowledge of me in the contents. It reads –

'My dear Fatayi,
    On behalf of my wife and myself, I congratulate you most heartily on your appointment as Chief Justice of Nigeria. The waiting has been long: nevertheless, the preferment is historic and richly deserved.

I wish you all the best, and pray that God grant you more than ever before the wisdom and courage to meet the demands of your high office.

Once again, heartiest congratulations.
    (signed)
OBAFEMI AWOLOWO'

I found the various congratulatory messages most encouraging in the arduous task which lay ahead. Little did I realise, however, that I would be the centre of controversy because of the decision which we handed down in respect of the first case over which I presided as Chief Justice.

A few weeks after I had been sworn-in as the Chief

153

Justice of Nigeria, I began to wonder whether I really wanted the job. Admittedly, I had the ambition of reaching the top in my chosen career and this new preferment is indeed the top. The Supreme Court, as one newspaper columnist rightly pointed out, would become known as 'the Fatayi-Williams Court'. Technically, of course, the Chief Justice is only the first among equals, but the post had definite prestige. He is the head of the Federal Judiciary, the third arm of the Federal Government. On the other hand, his vote in court stands no more than that of each of the other ten justices of the Court. However, that is not all there is to the post of Chief Justice. He also has the additional chores of administering the Court and of being involved in all the tedius little decisions involved in such administration. In addition, he has overall responsibility for the other Federal Courts – the Federal Court of Appeal and the Federal High Court.

The Chief Justice also oversees, as chairman, the work of such Commissions and Committees as the Federal Judicial Service Commission, the Legal Practitioners' Privileges Committee, the Judiciary Consultative Committee (a Committee of the national judiciary consisting of the President of the Federal Court of Appeal, the Chief Judge of the Federal High Court, the Chief Judges of the nineteen State High Courts, and a representative of the Grand Khadis of the Northern States), and the National Archives Committee. By virtue of his office, he is also a life member of the Body of Benchers of the Nigerian Bar, a body responsible for calling law students to the Nigerian Bar after they have passed the prescribed examinations set by the Nigerian Law School.

After many years as a justice of the Supreme Court, I have honestly come to the conclusion that in terms of job satisfaction, it is better to be a mere justice of the Court than to be the Chief Justice. In the former capacity, one's job is all law and no nonsense. Nevertheless, it is an appointment which nobody who has opted for a judicial career could or would refuse.

Added to all these was the early responsibility of presiding over the appeal against the decision of the Presidential Election Tribunal which had dismissed the petition of one of the presidential candidates against the election of Alhaji Shehu Shagari as the first executive President of the Federal Republic of Nigeria. The sequence of events leading to the hearing of the appeal is as follows.

The presidential election took place throughout the country on 8 August 1979. Five candidates contested the election. They were Chief Obafemi Awolowo of the Unity Party of Nigeria, Dr Nnamdi Azikiwe of the Nigeria People's Party, Mallam Aminu Kano of the People's Redemption Party, Alhaji Waziri Ibrahim of the Great Nigeria People's Party, and Alhaji Shehu Shagari of the National Party of Nigeria. Three days later, on 11 August to be precise, the Federal Electoral Commission (also known as FEDECO), after the votes of all the five candidates had been counted, declared that Alhahi Shehu Shagari was the successful candidate at the Presidential Election.

Being dissatisfied with the result of the election, Chief Obafemi Awolowo, the candidate of the Unity Party of Nigeria, petitioned against the election of Alhaji Shehu Shagari. The petition was brought under the Electoral Decree which made provisions for the conduct of all the five elections which took place between July and August 1979, including the presidential election.

In the said petition brought against Shehu Shagari (1st respondent), Alhaji Ahmadu Kurfi, the Electoral Officer of the Federation (2nd respondent), and F L O Menkiti, the Returning Officer for the Presidential Election (3rd respondent), Chief Awolowo stated that the election of Alhaji Shehu Shagari was invalid by reason of non-compliance with the provisions of section

155

34A(i) (c) (ii) in Part II of the Electoral Decree 1977. After referring to section 7 of the Electoral (Amendment) Decree 1978, he prayed –

'(i) that it may be determined that the said Alhaji Shehu Shagari was not duly elected or returned and that his election or return was void; and

(ii) that the 2nd and 3rd respondents be ordered to arrange for an election to be held in accordance with the provisions of section 34A (3) of the Electoral (Amendment) Decree 1978'.

The second prayer was abandoned during the hearing of the petition before the Presidential Election Tribunal.

The Tribunal which heard the petition consisted of Justices B O Kazeem, A I Aseme, and A B Wali, all justices of the Federal Court of Appeal. Justice B O Kazeem presided. Incidentally, Justice Kazeem is a Yoruba from Lagos State, Justice Aseme an Ibo from Imo State, and Justice Wali, a Hausa, from Kano State.

The Tribunal, after hearing evidence in support, dismissed the petition. It is significant to point out, at this juncture, that although Dr Nnamdi Azikiwe and Alhaji Waziri Ibrahim joined Chief Awolowo in condemning the conduct of the presidential election by FEDECO and rejecting the result in a strongly worded statement read by Dr Nnamdi Azikiwe at the Press Conference which was held in the Eko Hotel on 20 August 1979, it was only Chief Awolowo who filed an election petition on that same day. The other two candidates did not join him in the petition.

It was against this order of dismissal that Chief Awolowo had appealed to the Supreme Court. This appeal turned out to be my first major assignment after I was sworn-in as Chief Justice on 21 August 1979, the day after Chief Awolowo filed his appeal.

At the time the appeal was filed there were, apart from the Chief Justice, ten other justices of the Supreme Court. The ten were – Sir Udo Udoma, Justices

Sowemimo, Irikefe, Bello, Idigbe, Obaseki, Kayode Eso, Aniagolu, Nnamani and Uwais. Knowing how important the result of the appeal would be for the future peace and stability of the country and for the first civilian administration after fourteen years of military rule, I tried to include all available members of the court in the panel which was to hear the appeal. Unfortunately, this was not possible because Sir Udo Udoma, for personal reasons, the details of which a Chief Justice or presiding justice does not normally ask for, declined to sit. Justice Sowemimo was away in the United Kingdom undergoing medical treatment, while Justice Nnamani, apart from being responsible for the drafting of the provisions of the Decree which was being challenged, had been deployed, after being sworn-in as a justice of the Supreme Court, by the military administration, as the Federal Attorney-General and Commissioner for Justice. That left only the Chief Justice and seven justices. As the Court does not normally sit with an even number of justices, I decided that one of the seven justices would be dropped. The seven of us who heard the appeal, which under normal conditions, would have been heard by a bench consisting of the Chief Justice and four other Justices, were myself, Justices Ayo Irikefe, Muhammed Bello, Chike Idigbe, Andrews Obaseki, Kayode Eso and Muhammed Uwais. Any Nigerian would see, at a glance, that the panel, having regard to the justices available, had as wide an ethnic or a geographical spread as was possible in the circumstances.

Twenty-five lawyers led by Mr G O K Ajayi, appeared for Chief Awolowo at the hearing of the appeal on 17 September 1979. Alhaji Shehu Shagari was represented by Chief R O A Akinjide and eleven other lawyers, while the Chief Electoral Officer and the Returning Officer were both represented by two law officers. It must, I think, be emphasised that what the Supreme Court had to decide at the hearing of the appeal, and did decide, had nothing to do with any election malpractices. No evidence of corruption or of rigging was adduced before the Tribunal which heard the petition. The only matter canvassed before the Tribunal and with which the Supreme Court was concerned was the interpretation of certain provisions of the Electoral Decree. And that was what the Court did, basing its decision on the uncontradicted evidence which the Tribunal accepted. The evidence relates to the pattern of voting at the presidential election.

The relevant part of the main judgment dismissing the appeal, which was delivered by myself, reads –

'It is our view that in most countries with common law jurisdictions such as Nigeria, it is generally accepted that it is the function of the judiciary to interpret the law with the minimum of direction from the legislature as to how they should set about this task. Thus nearly all the principles, precepts and maxims of statutory interpretation are judge-made. Here are some examples. A statute should always be looked at as a whole, words used in a statute are to be read according to their meaning as popularly understood at the time the statute became law, a statute is presumed not to alter existing law beyond that necessarily required by the statute.

Some of those "canons" of interpretation take the form of broad general principles only. Consequently, a common feature of most of them is that they are of little practical assistance in settling doubts about interpretation in particular cases. This is partly due to vagueness, but also because, in many cases, where one canon appears to support a particular interpretation, there is another canon, often of equal status, which can be invoked in favour of an interpretation which could lead to a different result.

It is for the above reason that Maxwell's authoritative book on Interpretation of Statutes is not always of much assistance. Indeed, the work contains every conceivable interpretation to suit practically every point of view. We think that is why the learned author of the twelfth edition aptly observed in the Preface –

"Maxwell might well be sub-titled 'the practitioner's armoury'; it is, I trust not taking too cynical a view of statutory interpretation in general, and this work in particular, to express the hope that counsel putting forward diverse interpretations of some statutory provision will each be able to find in Maxwell *dicta* and illustrations in support of his case".

In the context of Nigeria, where the rate of promulgation of Decrees has been prolific during the last few years, it would be safe to adhere to the view once expressed by the late Lord Evershed MR that –

"the length and detail of modern legislation has undoubtedly reinforced the claim of literal construction as the only safe rule".

In the case in hand, legal authorities have been cited before us in support of one canon of interpretation or another when considering the meaning of the provisions of section 34A (1) (c) (ii) of the Electoral Decree. It has even been urged upon us, albeit without much success, to seek the aid of a well-known Nigerian scholar and applied mathematician. But at the end of the day, we must realise that we are interpreting a particular statute passed under special circumstances. For the purpose of the Decree under consideration, a Returning Officer, in our view, should be primarily concerned with the total number of votes cast by the voters in each of the 19 States of the Federation, bearing in mind that the entire Federation is each candidate's constituency. From the total number of votes cast throughout the country, he will identify the candidate who has the highest number of votes cast by the voters at the election. After this, he (the Returning Officer) will find the votes which this candidate has scored in each State. This has been done in Exh.T2.

It is at this stage that the Returning Officer ought to determine what is 2/3 of 19 States. This is a matter of law as it deals with the interpretation of the provisions of section 34A (1) (c) (ii) of the Decree. It is also relevant, we think, to point out that anybody called upon to interpret any kind of statute should not, for any reason, attach to its statutory provision, a meaning which the words of the statute cannot reasonably bear. If the words used are capable of more than one meaning, then the person interpreting the statute can choose between these meanings, but beyond that he must not go. (See *Jones v Director of Public Prosecutions* [1962] AC 635 at p.662). Thus, in *Nokes v Doncaster Amalgamated Collieries Ltd* [1940] AC 1014 (PC) at page 1022, Viscount Simon LC observed, rightly in our view, that –

"Judges are not called upon to apply their opinions of sound policy so as to modify the plain meaning of statutory words, but where, in construing general words the meaning of which is not entirely plain there are adequate reasons for doubting whether the legislature could have been intending so wide an interpretation as would disregard fundamental principles, then we may be justified in adopting a narrower construction".

Not only is the meaning of the general words used in section 34A plain enough, there is also no reason for doubting the intention of the Federal Military Government. The principles of construction enunciated above, and with which we entirely agree, take care of the permutation put forward by Professor Awojobi (1st witness for the appellant) and also of the other interpretation put on the words and figures used in the said section by learned counsel for the appellant.

This is precisely what the 3rd respondent has done in the case in hand and with unassailable justification, if we may say so, for the following reason. The Federal Military Government divided the Federation into nineteen States in 1976 by the States (Creation and Transitional Provisions) Decree (Decree No 12 of 1976). The Decree which came into force on 3 February 1976, also specified the geographical area of each of the nineteen States. Less than two years later, on 29 December 1977, to be precise, the same Government promulgated the Electoral Decree (No 73 of 1977), the original section 34 (2) (i) (b) of which contained the following words –

"he has not less than one-quarter of all the votes cast at the election in each of at least two-thirds of all the States within the Federation".

Although the section was later amended by the Electoral (Amendment) Decree (Decree No 32 of 1976) the above words were not amended, except for the deletion of the word "all" in the first line thereof, as they could have been amended, by adding a proviso using words similar to those used in paragraph 19 of Table C of Schedule 1 of the Companies Decree 1968 (Decree No 51 of 1968). After providing in the said paragraph that one-third of all the directors for the time being shall retire from office at the first annual general meeting of the company, the paragraph then went on to say that –

"if their number is not three or a multiple of three, *then the number nearest to one-third, shall retire from office*".

That being the case, the Federal Military Government must be deemed to know that two-thirds of 19 States will be twelve two-third States.

161

If the number thirteen which is the number nearest to two-thirds of a State had been intended, the Federal Military Government would have said so in clear terms. In any case, as between thirteen States and twelve two-thirds States, the figure of twelve two-thirds, considering all the circumstances, appears to us to be the intention of the Federal Military Government in the context of sub-paragraph (ii) of subsection (1) (c) of section 34A. Furthermore, it is, we think, fallacious to talk of fractionalisation of the physical land area of a State when the operative words of section 34A (1) (c) (ii) relate undoubtedly to the votes cast by the voters in the State at the election. It is also fallacious to talk of scaling down the votes cast for the 1st respondent in Kano State by one-third. That argument, if we may say so, overlooks the clear and unambiguous words of section 34A (1) (c) (ii) which provide FIRST for ascertaining the total number of votes cast for the 1st respondent by the voters of Kano State before comparing this figure obtained thereby with two-thirds of all the votes cast in Kano State in order to determine whether the votes received by him are not less than one-quarter of two-thirds of all the votes cast in Kano State.

The 3rd respondent, being a layman, has opted for a literal interpretation while the petitioner would want him to go into complicated mathematical calculation. But as Lord Simmons has rightly pointed out in *Magor and St Mellons Rural District Council v Newport Corporation* [1952] AC (HL) at p.191 –

"The duty of the court is to interpret the words that the legislature has used; those words may be ambiguous, but, even if they are, the power and duty of the court to travel outside them on a voyage of discovery are strictly limited".

Bearing all these in mind, and considering the divergent, but strong views urged upon us by learned counsel for all the parties as to the correct interpretation of the rather clumsily worded section which, to our mind, is nevertheless, devoid of any semantic ambiguity, we are not prepared to say that the 3rd respondent was in error in his interpretation of what constitutes two-thirds of nineteen states. Moreover, until election returns can be computerised in this country, the "mathematical canon of interpretation" put forward by Professor Awojobi (1st petitioner's witness) in his testimony before the Tribunal will remain impractical and legally unacceptable!

Quite apart from the compliance with the provisions of section 34A (1) (c) (ii) of the Decree as found by us, there is indisputable evidence –

(a) that the 1st respondent secured more votes throughout the country than each of the other four candidates;

(b) that he secured 772,206 votes more than those secured by the petitioner/appellant;

(c) that he scored at least 25% of the votes cast in each of twelve and two-thirds States out of the nineteen States in the Federation;

(d) that the country-wide votes referred to in (a) above are more geographically spread than those of any of the other four candidates;

(e) that even in the disputed votes of Kano State, the respondent secured 19.94% of the total votes cast in that State, while the petitioner/appellant secured only 1.23% of those votes. Exh. T2 refers;

(f) that the percentage of 19.94 scored by the 1st respondent in respect of the votes cast in the whole of Kano State falls short of 25% by only 5.06%.

In view of the above, there is no doubt that, even if we had found that there had been non-compliance with the said provisions, we would have invoked the provisions of section 111 subsection (1) of the Decree and held that the election, which in the present context means the election to the office of President, was conducted *substantially* in accordance with the provisions of section 34A (1) (c) (ii) which is within Part II of the Decree. Section 111 subsection (1) reads:–

> III (1). An election shall not be invalidated by reason of non-compliance with Part II of the Decree if it appears to the Tribunal having recognisance of the question that the election was conducted substantially in accordance with the provisions of the said Part II and that the non-compliance did not affect the result of the election.

In order to appreciate the far-reaching effect of the subsection (which is much wider in scope than the apparently similar section construed in *Morgan v Simpson* [1975] 1 QB 151 at pp.167–168), reference should also be made to the provisions of the preceding section 110 subsection (1) which read –

> 110 (1). An election may be questioned on any of the following grounds, that is to say –
> (a) that a person whose election is questioned was, at the time of the election, not qualified to be elected;
> (b) that the election was invalid by reason of corrupt practices *or non-compliance with the provisions of Part II of this Decree;*
> (c) that the respondent was, at the time of the election, not duly elected by a majority of lawful votes at the election;
> (d) that the petitioner was validly nominated but was unlawfully excluded from the election. [the underlining is ours].

A close look at the provisions of section 110 subsection (1) shows that, of all the stated grounds (five in all) on which a presidential election may be questioned, it is only when the petition is questioned on the ground of "non-compliance" with any of the provisions of Part II of the Decree that a Tribunal, and indeed this Court, can still dismiss the petition on the ground that –

> "the election was conducted substantially in accordance with the provisions of the said Part II and that the non-compliance did not affect the result of the election".

Finally, we would like to refer briefly to the concession made by the petitioner/appellant in the course of his address before the Tribunal that the second prayer in his petition was "otiose". Realising, as we do, that the word "otiose" means futile, not required, or serving no useful purpose, we do not see the real purpose of this appeal except, perhaps to enable this Court to interpret the words, percentage, and fraction, used in section 34A subsection (1) (c) (ii) of the Electoral Decree. Be that as it may, and for the reasons which we have highlighted in this judgment, we see no reason for disturbing the findings and conclusions of the Tribunal. The appeal therefore fails and it is dismissed. The decision of the Tribunal is affirmed'.

For six months, from the day following the day when the judgment was delivered, I was singled out for persistent attacks, laced with disgusting innuendoes by the columnists of newspapers controlled by or sympathetic to the Unity Party of Nigeria. Throughout these attacks, I 'kept my cool' and did not say a word. The culmination of these attacks came during the convention of the Unity Party of Nigeria held at the Eko Hotel, Lagos, in December 1979, and at which Chief Awolowo delivered an address attacking me and other government functionaries, including Alhaji Shehu Shagari, whom I, as Chief Justice, had sworn-in as the first Executive President of the Federal Republic of Nigeria on 1 October 1979. Chief Awolowo stated, in that address, that I was Alhaji Shehu Shagari's nominee for the post of Chief Justice.

In his reply to the attack on 12 December, 1979, General Olusegun Obasanjo, the Head of the Federal Military Government, from whom Alhaji Shehu Shagari took over the administration of the country on 1 October, observed –

'On the appointment of the Chief Justice, I will only repeat the fact which I am sure is well known to you, that the Supreme Military Council made the appointment. And I believe that all well-meaning Nigerians all over the country and outside who appreciated the need of the Judiciary and the worth of the present incumbent of the highest Judicial office in the land hailed the appointment and congratulated the appointee'.

Chief Awolowo, still dissatisfied, responded to General Obasanjo's reply on 17 December 1979, as follows –

'The second charge relates to the appointment of the new Chief Justice of Nigeria. In your subtlety, you have glossed over the inconvenient facts revealed. Instead you deliberately altered the particulars of offence to suit your defence. Nobody doubts the qualifications of Mr Justice Fatayi-Williams for elevation to the Chief Justiceship of Nigeria. I myself wrote to congratulate him on his appointment. That is not the issue which I raised in my address. Besides, I never said that someone else other than the Supreme Military Council made the appointment. What I said was that the appointment was rushed. Why not leave the vacancy unfilled until after October 1? I also contended that Alhaji Shagari was not only consulted, but also that he it was who chose Mr Justice Fatayi-

Williams from a list of candidates. You know the whole truth about this appointment, but you refuse to tell it in your letter. Do you still seriously maintain that the President could not be sworn-in unless a substantive Chief Justice of Nigeria was previously appointed? And now, you should be able to inform the Nigerian public what weighty issues of law you envisaged would arise between 21/8/79 and October 1 1979, and which only Mr Justice Fatayi-Williams could settle, bearing in mind that there were other Judges on the Supreme Court Bench who are as qualified as Mr Justice Fatayi-Williams in terms of learning, though not of seniority. I said in my address that the only weighty issues of law that could arise and which in fact had arisen were those raised in my election petition. You subtly left this weighty allegation untouched, and instead tried to shift the platform of contention to that of qualifications.

You and Alhaji Shagari considered three candidates – Chief Rotimi Williams, Dr Justice Udo Udoma, and Mr Justice Fatayi-Williams. The Nigerian public should be told why you left it to Alhaji Shehu Shagari to make a discretionary choice from among these three giants of the Bar and Bench, and then used the SMC as rubber stamp for Alhaji Shagari's decision. Moreso as, at the time Alhaji Shagari expressed his preference to you on 19/8/79 or 20/8/79, both you and Alhaji Shagari knew very well that I had filed an election petition challenging the validity of Alhaji Shagari's election, and that the matter might, more likely than not, eventually end up in the Supreme Court. In fact, at an informal meeting at Dodan Barracks, two days before FEDECO perfidiously declared Alhaji Shagari the winner, you did envisage this course of action.

Furthermore, another question which you omit to answer in your letter and which you must answer is this: Is it proper, legally and morally, that a respondent to an election petition, who has no constitutional right whatsoever to do so, should take part in the process of appointing the Chief Justice of Nigeria, let alone express preference for one from among these candidates when, at the time of the appointment, it was already known that the Chief Justice would preside over an appeal in which Alhaji Shagari might be appellant or respondent? It stands to reason that it was because you were inflexibly determined that, come what might, Alhaji Shagari was going to be installed President on October 1, that you allowed him to commit the unconstitutional abomination of choosing a new Chief Justice of Nigeria at a time when the validity of his election was *sub judice*. What did Nigeria gain by rushing the appointment? And what would it have lost by leaving the appointment to be made by the new President after October 1? We know a little though not enough of why Alhaji Shagari preferred Mr Justice Fatayi-Williams. Chief Rotimi Williams was rejected because he was said to have expressed a view identical with that of the Federal Attorney-General on "each of at least two-thirds of the nineteen States in the Federation". Dr Justice Udo Udoma was not liked because he was said to be so friendly with me that he practically ate most of his meals with me.

If these were the grounds for preference – I sincerely hope they are not – then the less said in this letter about the compelling logical inferences, the better. If these reasons were not the true ones, you would be doing public morality and the integrity of the Supreme Court Bench a world of good, if you could tell the people of this country why, with your acquiescence, Alhaji Shagari preferred Mr Justice Fatayi-Williams to Chief Rotimi Williams and Dr Justice Udo Udoma'.

The truth as to my appointment, as far as I am aware, is as I have described it earlier in this book. I was not aware, nor was I told, of any consultation between General Obasanjo and Alhaji Shehu Shagari over my appointment. It will, however, be recalled that Alhaji Shehu Shagari was declared to be the successful candidate at the presidential election on 11 August 1979. The Electoral Decree provided that any petition against the election must be filed within ten days of the declaration of the result. Until Chief Awolowo actually filed his election petition on 20 August 1979, which was the very last day on which he could have filed it, General Obasanjo could not assume that any of the unsuccessful candidates would petition against the result. It was, therefore, natural that he would discuss various matters concerning the handing over of power during those ten days with somebody who, at that time, had emerged as the President-elect. The government of the country could not and should not wait until Chief Awolowo and the other candidates had made up their minds whether they were going to file an election petition or not.

It was probably because of these discussions, which the gossip columnists wrote about at the time, that made Chief Awolowo come to the conclusion that my appointment must have been discussed. As I had said earlier, whether it was discussed or not, I did not, and still do not know. All I can say is that the last time I saw Alhaji Shehu Shagari until 29 September 1979 (two days before he was sworn-in by me) was some time in 1975 just before he left the Federal Military Government as the Federal Commissioner for Finance. The meeting was at one of the State Banquets in the Independence Hall at the Federal Palace Hotel in Lagos. All we did that evening was to say 'Hello' and shake hands. The next time I saw him was on 29 September when I went to explain to him in person that, in order to ensure the continuity of the Presidency, it was constitutionally desirable to swear-in the Vice-President first. I had heard that either he, or some of his political advisers, had certain misgivings about this procedure. We never discussed anything else. There was no need to.

It was therefore unfair, and unkind to say the least, for Chief Awolowo to have inferred, as he did in his address, that Alhaji Shehu Shagari could have seen me after my appointment and discussed certain matters with me. Chief Awolowo knows me and my family well enough. He also knows or ought to have known (I worked under him when he was the Premier of Western Nigeria in the fifties) that I hold him in very high esteem. He also knows, or ought to know, that the ruling force of my life was my supreme and undiluted dedication to the cause of justice according to law. He ought to know of my firm belief in the rule of law and my constant fear that once the rule of law is jettisoned, particularly in a developing country, anarchy will be the only beneficiary.

For an advocate of his pre-eminence at the Bar to make such a monstrous and unfounded allegation, just because he was not elected the President of this great country, without counting the cost, which might include the undermining of the faith which our people have in the judiciary, would not, I am sure, help his continuing ambition to become the President of the country. Six of us dismissed his appeal. Why did he have to pick on me so ruthlessly and give his supporters the untenable impression that the other five justices were mere rubber-stamps and merely signed the judgment which I delivered? His insult to them and their integrity, if he must know, was far greater than anything he had said or written about me. In none of his tirades did he attack the appointments of Justices Nnamani and Uwais or of Major-General Akinrinade, all of which were made by the same Federal Military Government around the same time as my appointment.

Some political commentators have observed that Chief Awolowo singled me out for attack because he could not conceive of a situation in which a fully-fledged Yoruba like me would give judgment against him. I, for my part, reject this observation. Only history can explain why a person like Chief Awolowo, who I know loves Nigeria so well, could do so much, because he had failed to win an elective office which the winner could only hold for four years before the next election, to destroy the very fabric, whether legislative, executive or judicial, of the very country over which he sought to rule. The whole episode was most disappointing. Happily, his boom, in this particular matter, lacks depth; or to put it in another way, his lightning brings no thunder. What was emotionally authentic at the time is now a forgotten foible.

Postscript

Looking back, it seems to me that, in their journey through life, men and women have nothing to fear as long as they make themselves the architects of their fates and the captains of their souls. I cannot, in this connection, improve on the observations made by Lord Birkett, a Lord of Appeal in Ordinary in England, when, after his retirement from the Bench, he was asked, in 1959, to recount briefly what he had learnt from life. This is what Lord Birkett said.–

'I have seen a good deal of human nature in my time. I have spent long years in the Court of Law as counsel and then as a judge, and that experience has taught me that men and women can shape their own lives by their own efforts and determination.

I have seen many a young man pull himself together and foresake evil ways by his resolute purpose and endeavour. I am not forgetting the enormous part that heredity and environment play – the special equipment with which people are born, or the state of life to which they are called – and whilst these things may determine the ultimate course of life, I yet hold firmly to the belief that what men and women make of their lives depends very largely upon themselves.

171

The world has changed a great deal in my life-time and we must all adapt ourselves to change if we can; but I still think there are some changeless things in the world that make or mar our happiness. Let me therefore conclude with a few of the ideas I have learned from my own life. I think that men and women who can choose their job, and find a daily pleasure in doing it, are fortune's favourites; that a happy home life is the very greatest of human blessings; that there is infinite wisdom in the old words "whatsoever thy hand findeth to do, do it with thy might"; that it is wise to have a hobby of some kind, and if it is a useful hobby, so much the better; that it is the highest wisdom to make friends, and to take every kind of trouble to keep the friendships in repair, particularly as you grow older; that *excess in all things* is to be avoided; that it is wise to keep one's word, and not to break promises; that a sense of public duty should be cultivated, if only as a safeguard against selfishness; and that it is wise to keep the mind alert by reading and by all the agencies, such as television and radio, that now exert themselves for our benefit.

I think it is wise to realise the value of a margin in all things, and not only in money matters; and not to spend too much time in seeking mere pleasure; and not to live for the moment only. . . .

In the end, it is *life* that teaches us all'.

Over the years, I have a lot to be thankful for. I have learned to live quietly amidst the noise and haste; I have found a way to be on good terms with all persons without surrendering the basic principles guiding my life. I have tried to speak the truth as I see it, quietly and clearly, listening, at the same time, to others, even the dull and the ignorant. I have maintained and sustained the independence of the judiciary irrespective of the consequences to my own career and future prospects. I have learned to just be myself, not comparing myself with others. This is to avoid becoming vain and bitter because there will always be greater and lesser persons than myself.

In the course of my career, I have found that the stability of any institution rests NOT on the inordinately ambitious, the impatient, the sharp-elbowed go-getters jockeying for places, pushing their way to the top, clamourously envious of other people's success. To my mind, it rests on those who practise the unspectacular and, at the present time, the totally unfashionable virtue of inner contentment, disinterested loyalty, patience, and satisfaction in one's chosen work for its own sake, irrespective of status. Everything in our aggressively acquisitive profit-obsessed society is, admittedly, loaded against that.

I have learned how to enjoy both my plans and my achievements. I take kindly to the counsel of the years. I nurture the strength of spirit which has always shielded me from the vicissitudes of life and the swinging barometer of fortune.

I believe that with all its sham drudgery, treachery, and temporary setbacks, it is still a beautiful world, a world in which we can all strive to maintain the rule of law and sustain and protect the fundamental rights of all its citizens. All things considered, life has been kind to me. There are, indeed, very few regrets although I must admit that there have been many minor irritations. I have succeeded far beyond my wildest expectations.

Finally, I am glad for the opportunity to be counted among the standard-bearers of the administration of justice in post-war Nigeria and to be able to reach the very top of my chosen career. The sense of fulfilment has made the period of waiting worthwhile!

10 The President reflects

On Friday 19 February 1982, almost two-and-a-half years after I took office as the Chief Justice of Nigeria, Alhaji Shehu Shagari, the President of the Federal Republic of Nigeria, gave a private dinner in honour of the Judiciary Consultative Committee. The Members of this Committee are the Chief Judge of each of the 19 States of the Federation, the Chief Judge of the Federal High Court, the President of the Federal Court of Appeal, and the Chief Justice of Nigeria who is the Chairman. The Grand Kadi of Sokoto State also represents all the Grand Kadis of the ten Northern States on the Committee. The Committee is purely consultative; it meets, at least, four times a year and at other times as and when necessary. Its members exchange views and ideas on the various ways and means of improving the administration of the Judiciary of Nigeria in all its ramifications, and of enhancing the quality and speed of justice available to all our peoples.

In addition to all the members of the Judiciary Consultative Committee, also present at the dinner were, among others, Dr Joseph Wayas – the distinguished President of the Senate, all the Justices of the Supreme Court of Nigeria, some of the Justices of the Federal Court of Appeal, and the Attorney-General of the Federation and Minister of Justice.

The President of the Federal Republic of Nigeria spoke at the dinner about the Judiciary headed by me. Without any doubt, he spoke from the heart that night. It was a speech to remember, an objective analysis of the

174

role which the Judiciary in Nigeria has been playing since he took office as President in October 1979. This is what he said –

'All of us – the three arms of government – have just over two years experience in the Presidential system of Government and in the operation of our new Constitution. During these two years, each arm has undergone some critical tests in the process of operating our new Constitution.

From records, the Executive arm has been taken to court a number of times. The Legislative arm has similarly been dragged to court. In each case Your Lordships gave your verdict. I am glad to say before you that we, on whom those verdicts have been passed, have always respected your pronouncements. We have by so doing, demonstrated to you, to our people and to the whole world, not only our respect for, but also our commitment to, the Rule of Law. We have shown our determination to live by it. It is on record that even where we had cause to feel dissatisfied, we made sure that, in exercising our right of appeal, we strictly adhered to the rules and procedures as laid down by law. We have by our actions affirmed our commitment to the principle of separation of powers, particularly the independence of the Judiciary, which is central to our democratic system of Government.

Indeed, there are people who regard those citizens of our country who challenge the constitutionality of certain actions of Government as bad citizens who are obstructing the progress of the nation. I want to assure you that I do not hold or share this view. On the contrary, I believe that by freely exercising their fundamental right to take matters to court for constitutional interpretation, such people are helping us to consolidate the Constitution. In every case where the Supreme Court is called upon to give an interpretation on one provision or other in the Constitution it is creating history and helping posterity because, should similar disputes arise at any time in future, there will be legal precedents to cite. This is one of the reasons why I have never nursed a grudge against, nor quarrelled with anyone for going to court to seek constitutional interpretation of any of our actions. I know of course that there may be a few whose motive for taking Governments to court is far from genuine. Their desire may be to obstruct or embarrass or ridicule the Government. I am never disheartened, not even by such ill-wishers of this country. My reason is simply because I have the greatest respect, trust and confidence in our judiciary, and respect for the rights of all Nigerians under the Constitution.

I believe members of our judiciary are mature and are worthy of this respect. I believe they can and do always pass judgments without fear or favour. This I regard as one of the great blessings showered by God on our country. We are extremely lucky in being able to evolve, over the 20 years of our independence, a judiciary that is truly independent, a judiciary that is honest and a judiciary that has set standards for the rest of Africa to follow. Indeed ours is comparable to the best in the world. So if I say I am proud of Nigeria's judiciary I believe I am saying aloud the mind of the people of this country. One only needs to travel to some other parts of the developing world to be so convinced. Our respect for the integrity and impartiality of Nigeria's judiciary must therefore be maintained.

My Lords, in ensuring that this great confidence which your institution enjoys from all of us and the general public is not weakened, you must be prepared to set further examples which will strengthen that confidence. Your predecessors, and indeed yourselves, have worked hard and relentlessly in order to win this confidence for the judiciary of this land. You cannot entertain or do anything that will undermine that confidence or ruin it. In these days of great moral, social, economic and political temptations, this task of maintaining your tradition with the required dignity, this task of remaining part and parcel of the society but without mingling too much with it, is not easy. But then, it is a task that must be done if our country is to survive and be respected.

As the three arms of Government, the Constitution has created an atmosphere and provided an opportunity for us to work together, each with its limited autonomy. We check and balance one another in the course of discharging our duties. The main function of the judiciary is to protect the citizens from a wrong and arbitrary exercise of power. This is regardless of the source of that power. Power that is unchecked is power that corrupts. Indeed, the Judiciary, as the final arbiters of our Constitution, has tremendous powers. But as we all know even this power is not absolute. I am happy to note that Nigeria's judiciary provides itself with an additional self-imposed mechanism to ensure the non-absoluteness of its power. They certainly deserve our congratulations. We are no doubt fortunate and do thank God for giving us this good fortune. We have, in Your Lordships, gentlemen of character and integrity. We have firm but humane gentlemen, good citizens who believe in their country and are willing to contribute to its progress, unity, peace and stability.

I know there are no cushions on the Bench. Only dedication and hard work, backed by integrity and loyalty to the nation, can get one through. But I also know that those who are there now possess the necessary talent, tact and courage to sail through with honour and with colours. The challenge before us is gigantic but it is one that has to be met. Let us continue to face it for the sake of the nation that we are building and for the sake of the land that we love. For sure the day will come when we shall reap the fruit of this common endeavour.

Finally, my Lords, Distinguished Ladies and Gentlemen, by way of simple reminder, let me draw our attention to the fact that we are trustees, entrusted with the lives and destinies of millions. We dare not betray such sacred trust for the fulfilment of personal desires. I sincerely appreciate your role and cooperation. It is the existence of a few like you who put the interest of our nation above all else that encourages me to fight on so that this nation may survive.

God remains the final judge of our motives and our deeds. With His Blessing and Guidance we shall overcome'.

All I can say about these reflections of Mr President is that they mark yet another significant milestone in my journey through life. Given the necessary good health and staying power, the end of the journey may still not be in sight!

Index